# Rhetorical Strategies for Composition

# Rhetorical Strategies for Composition

## Cracking an Academic Code

### Second Edition

Karen A. Wink

ROWMAN & LITTLEFIELD

*Lanham • Boulder • New York • London*

Published by Rowman & Littlefield
An imprint of The Rowman & Littlefield Publishing Group, Inc.
4501 Forbes Boulevard, Suite 200, Lanham, Maryland 20706
www.rowman.com

6 Tinworth Street, London SE11 5AL, United Kingdom

British Library Cataloguing in Publication Information Available

**Library of Congress Cataloging-in-Publication Data**

Names: Wink, Karen A., author.
Title: Rhetorical strategies for composition : cracking an academic code /
    Karen A. Wink.
Other titles: Cracking an academic code
Description: Second edition. | Lanham : Rowman & Littlefield, [2020] |
    Revised edition of: Cracking an academic code : rhetorical strategies
    for composition, 2016. | Includes bibliographical references and index. |
    Summary: "Rhetorical Strategies for Composition: Cracking an Academic
    Code is a worktext designed for composition students to apply rhetorical
    theory in their writing"—Provided by publisher.
Identifiers: LCCN 2020035834 (print) | LCCN 2020035835 (ebook) | ISBN
    9781475857306 (paperback) | ISBN 9781475857313 (epub)
Subjects: LCSH: English language—Composition and exercises. | English
    language—Rhetoric—Study and teaching.
Classification: LCC LB1576 .W4895 2020 (print) | LCC LB1576 (ebook) | DDC
    372.62/3—dc23
LC record available at https://lccn.loc.gov/2020035834
LC ebook record available at https://lccn.loc.gov/2020035835

♾™ The paper used in this publication meets the minimum requirements of American National Standard for Information Sciences—Permanence of Paper for Printed Library Materials, ANSI/NISO Z39.48-1992.

*To Cameron, Donovan, Lily, and Jake whose brightness shines in my life.*

# Contents

# Acknowledgments

Special thanks to my editor Dr. Tom Koerner and associate editor Carlie Wall, for their guidance and support. An extra special thanks to Dr. Jeanne Fahnestock, Dr. Faye Ringel, Dr. Kim Parker for endorsements and editorial guidance. An extra, extra special thanks to my students for their inspiration and contributions to this text.

# Introduction

College writing assignments may as well be written in code—instructors' comments as well! "Insufficient analysis"; "close paraphrase = plagiarism"; "pronoun-agreement problems"; "overuse of passive voice"—what do these comments mean?

You have successfully followed assignment instructions in the past, but you may have wondered, "Why this insistence on a thesis?" "Why an introductory paragraph?" "Why use ethos, pathos, and logos in an argument?" "Why certain formats?" This text will answer these questions of yours and, perhaps, lead you to ask more questions—writing, after all, is a complex, yet rewarding, process.

It is no wonder academic writing resembles a code—some of the vocabulary is 2,500 years old (in Greek or Latin, at that!). While your Biology 101 class is unlikely to be based on the understanding of the biology of Aristotle, his philosophy and his theories of writing and reading remain the basis of English instruction.

You are already successful readers and writers, or you would not be holding this text. Now you can become reflective and masterful readers of academic documents and writers of essays and research papers, regardless of your major or intended career. Your undergraduate instructors assume you have learned how to read and write competently. But what if you need a review of, say, paraphrasing, revising, or figures of speech? This text can help you to refresh your understanding of these and other tools of language. This text can serve as a supplement to a course reader and as an aid in writing assignments.

The challenges involved in making the transition from high school to college English classes and writing cannot be underestimated. Look around your class—classmates are likely to have come from different schools and backgrounds. The goal of First-Year Composition is to access everyone's background knowledge from diverse English courses and focus on the goal of writing sound arguments—the basis of all college writing.

This text's title, *Rhetorical Strategies for Composition*, contains the word "rhetoric." The "rh" in "rhetoric" informs us that the word—and consequently, the art of rhetoric itself—is ancient, nearly unchanged from Aristotle's Greek. Why study such an ancient art? Citizens of the twenty-first century need more than ever to understand the techniques of persuasion: In an era of information overload and constant communication, we need to evaluate the validity of arguments and the credibility of those who are trying to persuade us to listen, buy, or vote. College students, especially, need to think critically and to demonstrate their ability to persuade others in speech and—more frequently—in writing.

The following chapters are based upon Aristotle's theory of rhetoric, as adapted by Connors and Corbett in *Classical Rhetoric for the Modern Student* and by other twentieth-century rhetorical and composition theorists. The technical vocabulary of argument includes not only Greek-derived words but also expressions we use often. The goal is for you to view all aspects of composition and conventions as "means of persuasion" (qtd. in Kennedy 3); this book focuses on these "means" by providing interconnected chapters that present strategies for laying out effective arguments.

## ARGUMENTATION

When "Googling" synonyms for the word "argument," these words come up: quarrel, fight, disagreement, dispute, row, spat, and squabble. But these words don't capture the meaning we have in mind—an argument, in the context of this book, is a piece of persuasive writing that is based on rational thinking.

## INTRODUCTION

- What is arguable? Essentially any topic to which we can apply critical thinking.
- What is generally not a "winnable" argument with people? Personal taste, beliefs, and faith.

We study classical rhetorical form not to emulate past rhetors, but rather to have a common foundation for understanding the historic arguments of the past and the best arguments of our own time. Much has changed in the thousands of years since argument was formalized, but much—surprisingly—has remained the same.

While analyzing any act of speech or writing, you must consider what is called the "rhetorical triangle." All the elements of this triangle find a place in the question, "Who is trying to convince whom or what, and in what circumstances?" As you use this book, keep in mind the following overarching principles contained in it:

- Reading and writing are connected experiences involving the power of words.
- All writing can be considered to be arguments or as efforts at persuasion because a writer makes choices and "sells" ideas. Think about this statement from the Talmud, a central Rabbinic Jewish book: "We do not see things as they are, we see them as we are." In other words, all ideas come from somewhere, and that somewhere is us, the writers who think creatively and critically, and then make choices.
- Persuasion refers not to manipulation, but to reasoned, strategic "thinking-on-paper" in a bid to channel events or action in a fair, advantageous direction. In general, everyone, including your audience members, is persuaded by what is advantageous.
- The words "audience" and "readers" are used interchangeably. Though audience can refer to readers, listeners, or viewers, for the purposes of this text, the main reference is to readers.
- Since this text is geared toward First-Year Composition, though many of the strategies are appropriate for Advanced Placement Language and Composition courses also it follows the style manual of the Modern Language Association (MLA), a style manual that students are expected to adhere to in First-Year Composition and other English courses.

Each chapter presents interconnected strategies used in sequence—starting with an explanation of rhetoric and the rhetorical situation, and building an understanding of the "roads" of composition that lead to a firmer grasp of argument.

As you use this text, liken your writerly self to a tour guide who takes travelers around a new city: your readers, like tourists, share some knowledge and assumptions, but need you to provide context, new information, and expert analysis. Like the tourists, your readers may be bored or uninterested—it will be up to you to invite them to read, to encourage them to continue reading, and to lead them from idea to idea in a way that reflects clear thinking and logical development.

But how can you be an effective tour guide unless you have done your research and know your way around that new city?—this in our context being academic writing. Let this text be your *Lonely Planet Guide*—a book which reveals the secrets of its instructors, and which helps you to speak their language.

## WEBSITE RECOMMENDATIONS FOR RHETORICAL ANALYSIS

www.americanrhetoric.org (bank of famous speeches)

www.archives.gov/education/lessons (National Archives site; links to historical documents to analyze rhetorically)

*Chapter 1*

# Rhetoric

## ESSENTIALS

*What is the original definition of rhetoric?* "An ability to see the available means of persuasion in any case," according to Aristotle, the ancient Greek philosopher and "inventor of formal logic" (qtd. in Kennedy 4, 35). Aristotle used the term "means," which in modern times, refers to a writer's tools and strategies.

*What is a modern definition of rhetoric?* To persuade others to understand and accept our arguments; to evaluate the legitimacy of others' arguments trying to persuade us. Rhetoric is also. . .

- a guide to realize why words are worth noticing
- a practical art
- a way of arranging words
- a way of supplying words
- how a writer's choices influence an argument
- how an argument is composed
- strategies to build convincing arguments
- what makes an argument effective or ineffective

*Why is rhetoric a misinterpreted word?* Rhetoric is an often misused word with a negative connotation. Some believe rhetoric refers to using words to mislead or manipulate an audience unjustly. For example, public figures may say: "Don't listen to all that rhetoric" or "The rhetoric of the campaign trail" or "She spoke a lot of rhetoric but did not provide solutions to the real problems." Rhetoric, however, is not necessarily spoken or written words, but the way in which the words are arranged and expressed.

*How is rhetoric a strategic act?* Rhetoric is not a negative act, but a strategic one. The results of these strategies are effective arguments based on the writer's choices. Reasonable, fair-minded voices express

these arguments, and are typically seen as qualified ones by the audiences.

*What is an example of rhetoric in daily life?* If you were asked by the principal or dean to take photos of sports teams at your school, and he or she said, "Make our teams look positive this week" or "Make our teams look negative this week," that's rhetoric. Here is a different sort of explanation from George Orwell, author of *1984* and *Animal Farm*:

> Propaganda in some form or other lurks in every book, that every work of art has a meaning and a purpose—a political, social and religious purpose—that our aesthetic judgements are always coloured by our prejudices and beliefs.

Orwell's argument suggests that every "work of art" or work of literature has a rhetorical meaning and purpose, which is the basis of this text.

*Briefly, what is the history behind classical-modern rhetoric?* In ancient Greece, speakers—called orators or rhetors—were leaders who influenced the citizens who participated in the first democracy. In addition to Aristotle, other leaders and philosophers—Plato and Socrates—and later Cicero in Rome, treated speeches as opportunities to educate, praise, blame, argue, and protest. They played a central role in shaping political thinking—similar to presidential state-of-the union or senator's campaign speeches. Since the ancient leaders had only one means of communication—speeches or orations—which could not be revised, they prepared well for their public performances.

Their orations served more than just practical purposes: they were strategic. In other words, they not only delivered the words, but worked the language to

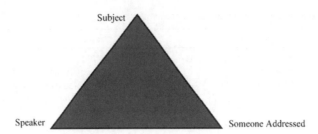

**Figure 1.1   Basic Rhetorical Situation.**

persuade the citizens and achieve some sort of effect. To create this effect, Aristotle provided a set of strategies for a rational argument. In these arguments, Aristotle pointed out that "a speech [situation] consists of three things: a speaker and a subject on which he speaks and someone addressed" (qtd. in Kennedy 47).

Many centuries later, in 1965, English professors Edward P. J. Corbett and Robert J. Connors adapted Aristotle's system in *Classical Rhetoric for the Modern Student.* They explained, "The so-called 'communications triangle' is frequently used as a graphic representation of the components of the rhetorical act: speaker/writer, subject-matter, listener/reader, and text"(2).

Since that time, there have been other versions of the rhetorical triangle, including the following adapted for purposes of this text.

All strategies in chapters 1–10 trace back to this triangle, more commonly referred to as a rhetorical situation, that is, an act of persuasion. As a writer, your goal is to make your words respond to the situation that surrounds your piece of writing so as to achieve your purpose and satisfy your audience. The seven elements include the following:

- Writer: Who is writing?
- Topic: What is the subject?
- Thesis: What is at issue?
- Audience: Who is reading?
- Text: Where?
- Context: When? Where?
- Purpose: Why?

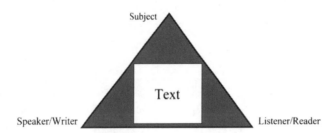

**Figure 1.2   Basic Rhetorical Situation.**

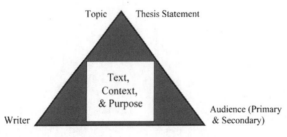

**Figure 1.3   Basic Rhetorical Situation.**

**Table 1.1   Comparison of the Rhetorical Triangle: Classical-Modern**

| Aristotle | Connors & Corbett | Modern Adaptation (Used in this text) |
| --- | --- | --- |
| Speaker | Speaker/Writer | Writer |
| Subject | Subject matter | Topic/Thesis statement |
| Someone addressed | Listener/Reader | Audience (primary and secondary) |
| [Oration] | Text | Text, context, and purpose |

All elements of the rhetorical triangle answer the question, "Who is trying to convince whom of what and when?"

*What are some of the other terms related to the rhetorical situation?*

- *Chronos* (Greek for chronology): time in a linear fashion
- Diction: word choice
- *Kairos* (Greek for right time): the right time and opportunity to convey a message; capitalizing upon a political, social, or economic time to put forth an argument
- *Occasio* (Latin for occasion): the optimal occasion
- Rhetor: writer or speaker putting forth an argument
- Syntax: sentence structure

*What is important to know about writing as you begin using this text?*

1. Writing is a complex thinking exercise that is
   - meant to be read
   - a process of discovery
   - an activity that takes energy and determination
   - a translation of thinking into coherent expression
2. Writing is using and understanding the power of words, that is, what words "do." Here are some of the things that words "do"
   - affect social change
   - bore us
   - commemorate an occasion
   - enrich our lives
   - express opinions
   - injure feelings
   - pay tribute to somebody
   - uplift our moods
3. Writing is rewriting—as many great writers have observed. Revision, or "re-envisioning," allows for more possibilities: ideas and ways of expressing the ideas that are being conveyed more fully. Revision is not unique to writing—painting, building furniture, running, fishing, playing chess, and many other such activities

require revision and involve transformation and adaptation. Each of these activities is a process that takes energy, concentration, and trial and error as well as "fits-and-starts." What is your North Star or passion?

Ask yourself: Why are my words worth noticing? Consider this a starting point.

*What is a definition of "text"?*

A useful definition is from *Advanced Placement Language and Composition* document:

- "any cultural product that can be 'read'-meaning not just consumed and comprehended but investigated. This includes fiction, non-fiction, poetry, political cartoons, fine art, photography, performances, fashion, cultural trends, and much more" (38).
- Connect terms "rhetoric" and "text"—all texts present arguments that we write or read.

Other Versions of the Rhetorical Situation (Triangle)

*Which version is common in Advanced Placement Composition and Language?*

SOAPSTone

**S** = Speaker (Whose voice is heard in the writing?)
**O** = Occasion (When did the surrounding event(s) take place? What was the Kairos?)
**A** = Audience (Who is the immediate group of people to whom the writing is aimed? Who is part of the wider group to whom the writing is also aimed?)
**P** = Purpose (Why is the writer writing about this topic?)
**S** = Subject (What is the main topic?)
**t** = Tone (What is the writer's attitude toward the topic?)

("apcentral.collegeboard")

*Which version is a "Model of Argumentation"?* The Toulmin model is

### Exercise 1
What are similarities and differences among the three versions? Explain.

### Exercise 2
Which model fits the rhetorical situation of your writing assignment? How will you apply model in part or all of your assignment?

## AUDIENCE

*Why is it important to consider your audience?* Writing is meant to be read. To this end, write while keeping your audience in mind by attending to their interests, engaging them, respecting their views, and writing coherent, legible prose. Prior to drafting papers, consider writing an audience analysis— this should help you to make important decisions about thesis, background, and evidence. Make a list of audience characteristics. Think about why the audience is reading your paper: to learn? to affect change? to refute? Then, tailor your writing to your audience—your writing should not seem remote or mismatched with their characteristics. Think about something you have read that was dry and dull; chances are the writer forgot about his or her readers who wanted to gain knowledge from the article.

*What is the difference between a primary audience and a secondary audience?* Your primary audience are the decision-makers—those who are invested in the topic you are writing about and who can affect change. They are most interested in the presented or finished draft. Your secondary audience are the others who are interested and influenced by the argument. Your secondary audience can also be the instructor and the peers of your class—they are also invested in your topic, but more so in the process of working toward a final version of the paper. In a classroom setting, imagining a "real" audience that transcends the classroom may seem like an exercise in artificiality, but there is value in this as it helps you to prepare for writing in your career.

## Toulmin Model of Argumentation

1. *Claim*: position or assertion; reasserted as conclusion
2. *Grounds:* supporting evidence
3. *Warrant:* key points connecting grounds to claim.
4. *Backing*: reasons supporting warrant
5. *Rebuttal/Reservation:* counter points to the claim
6. *Qualification*: constraints or limits of claim, warrant, and backing.

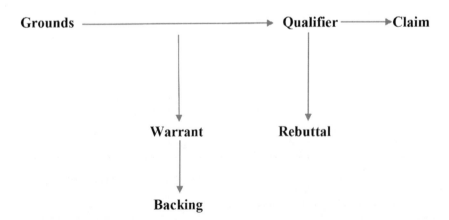

**Figure 1.4   Toulmin Model of Argumentation.**                    (owl.purdue.edu.../toulmin-argument.html)

**Table 1.2 Audience Characteristics**

*What are the characteristics of audience members to consider?*

| | |
|---|---|
| Age range | Geographical location |
| Background knowledge | Interests |
| Beliefs on topic | Race/ethnicity |
| Careers | Religious affiliation |
| Education | Socioeconomic class |
| Gender | Values |

*Note*: When writing a paper, your job is to give the "illusion" of a real experience and enter into a pledge of good faith with the audience.

*What is important to determine about your audience?* When determining the audience of a speech or published article, contemplate that a writer may have selected more than one primary and/or secondary audience. For instance, the president speaking at a college graduation may have two primary audiences: graduates and the press; secondary audiences could be friends, families, and other citizens who are listening to or have access to the speech. The needs of primary audiences align with the writer's purpose.

*What does it mean to write for an audience?* This means that you must have a strong consideration of readers who will experience your writing—this will involve an examination of the readers' views/ biases, feelings, backgrounds, vested interests, and receptivity. Since your writing (except for the self, e.g., personal journals) is meant to be read by others, it is worth your time to reflect on your audience and to attempt to connect with them, and to ensure that your text responds to the rhetorical situation.

*Do the majority views of your audience at the outset reflect support for your stances?* Will you "preach to the choir," engage undecided mindsets, or face a resistant, even hostile, audience? When you face an adverse audience, the challenge to establish credibility and sway their opinions is greater. Sometimes, this places a special onus or responsibility on your shoulders to think carefully about the needs of your audience. For instance, an undecided audience needs more information of pros/cons prior to decision-making. A hostile audience needs facts and reasoning, rather than opinion-based, emotionally charged information, for its hostility to be diffused and for its members to listen to your argument.

*What does it mean to write for an unintended audience?* In today's online environment, postings of many types—articles, blogs, commentary, e-mails, tweets, and so forth—can reach audiences worldwide. It is impossible to know who will read which postings; therefore, the Internet allows all sorts of expressions—some of them private—to become public property. To address this issue, ensure you are comfortable with the idea that

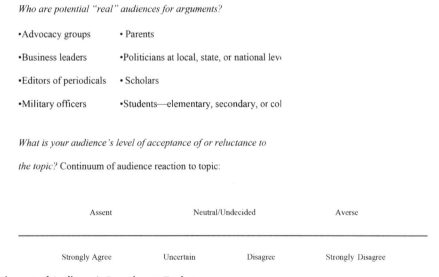

*Who are potential "real" audiences for arguments?*

| | |
|---|---|
| •Advocacy groups | • Parents |
| •Business leaders | •Politicians at local, state, or national lev |
| •Editors of periodicals | • Scholars |
| •Military officers | •Students—elementary, secondary, or col |

*What is your audience's level of acceptance of or reluctance to the topic?* Continuum of audience reaction to topic:

| Assent | Neutral/Undecided | Averse | |
|---|---|---|---|
| Strongly Agree | Uncertain | Disagree | Strongly Disagree |

**Figure 1.5 Continuum of Audience's Reaction to Topics.**

*"O.K., but what I'm about to tell you does not leave this news cycle."*

**Figure 1.6**   © **The New Yorker Collection, 2014.** Paul Noth. From cartoonbank.com. All rights reserved.

unintended audiences may read your postings. As the above cartoon shows, audiences may be beyond one's sphere of influence.

*What are your audience's expectations of you?* If your audience is negatively predisposed toward your arguments, try to uncover their objections and address them directly and honestly. Explain why the objections are invalid or less important than the arguments you have put forward in support of your stances. In your writing, include the objections first, then make your recommendation(s). Strive to build trust and cooperation with your audience. Seek common ground and stay professional—in other words, be flexible and fair-minded. To avoid alienating your audience, acknowledge several perspectives—rather than only your own—on the topic. It is important to concede to an opposing view and then refute its perceived weaknesses. Though the audience may initially be unconvinced, they may accept your argument upon reflection.

*When do you need to adjust diction and tone for different audiences?* This depends on the relationship you have with your audience: Are they your friends? Are they members of your family? Do they include your boss, director, supervisor, or instructor? And your purpose—is it to persuade, to inform, to explain, or to narrate? There may be other purposes, such as, to entertain or to vent, but they tend to fall under the main purposes.

This also depends on the format—for example, text, e-mail, paper, memo, cover letter, and lab report. Texting and posting on social media are considered the most informal, while e-mail is less so.

### Example 1

President Reagan's address, "The Space Shuttle *'Challenger* Tragedy'"

Primary audience: American adults and children; secondary audience: challenger astronauts and their families, and NASA employees.

Purpose: To memorialize a tragic event in American history.

Context: Oval Office; January 28, 1986.

Thesis statement describing the rhetorical situation of President Reagan's address:

During a national tragedy, President Reagan delivered a speech to Americans in which he paid respect to the *Challenger* crew and those closely associated with them. Additionally, he affirmed the significance of the NASA Space Program for future endeavors.

The full text of President Reagan's speech can be found at americanrhetoric.org.

**Table 1.3   Correspondence with Different Audiences**

| Audience | Text | Purpose | Level of Formality |
|---|---|---|---|
| Editor/Editorial Board of Newspaper or Journal | E-mail | To persuade | Formal |
| Instructor | E-mail | To inform | More formal |
| Job Supervisor | E-mail | To inform | More formal |
| Roommate | Email | To explain | More informal |
| Cousin | Text | To narrate | Informal |
| Friends | Posting on social media | To inform | Informal |

*Exercise 3*

Identify the primary audience of the following audiences:

1. A politician and his or her media advisers developing Facebook campaign messages.
2. A city newspaper reporter who is writing an article on a dedication of a school in the name of a beloved retired principal.
3. A chemist writing a laboratory report.
4. An advertiser creating an ad for a brand of children's vitamins.
5. A novelist writing a horror novel for fans of Halloween.
6. A high school student writing a research paper on benefits of hybrid cars.

*Exercise 4*

Audience analysis of a published piece:

Where does the article or writing appear? What is the credibility of the publication and the author? What is the author's topic? thesis statement?

Audience:

- Background knowledge: What is assumed about the audience's knowledge of the topic? What are the values of the audience?
- Pronoun usage: Does the writer use inclusive pronouns such as "we" or us" to make it seem as though the writer is part of the audience? Or does the writer directly address an organization or a group of people, such as the Town Council or human rights activists?
- Focus: What does the writer emphasize? advocate?

- Diction: Does the writer use words or jargon used specifically by professionals in a particular field (e.g., environmentalists)?
- Style: What is the level of formality or informality of the writing?

Audience: Based on your answers to the questions above, draw a conclusion on: Who is the primary audience? Who is the secondary audience? Which features of this argument are persuasive?

*Exercise 5*

Write a post, a text, and e-mails to various audiences on the following topic:

Topic: Scheduling a time to meet or rescheduling a meeting.

Questions

- What adjustments did you make in diction, in tone, and in terms of format?
- Why did you make various adjustments?

## TEXTS, CONTEXTS, AND PURPOSES

### Texts

*Which types of writing will you learn in your academic courses?* All types of academic writing are arguments because you are "selling" your ideas. You are making choices about information to include (or exclude!) in your arguments. There are various types of academic writing—each with its own format and each considered a text that your audience will interpret.

*Example 2*
*Academic Writing*

**Table 1.4  Academic Writing**

| Analytical papers | E-mails | Evaluations | Reports |
|---|---|---|---|
| Business plans | Essay exams | Legal briefs | Summaries |
| Critiques/reviews | Expository papers | Policy briefs | Synthesis papers |

## Contexts

*What is important to consider about the context of your academic writing?* Since your writing is situated, that is, taking place in a slice of time, it is worth your time to reflect on where (and to whom) you will submit your writing.

*Example 3*
Contexts

**Table 1.5  Contexts**

| Alumni magazine | Course assignment |
|---|---|
| Blogs | Journal with articles written by undergraduates |
| College newspaper | University/college website |

## Purposes

*What is meant by a writing purpose?* When starting the writing process, ask yourself: Why are you writing this text? The more clarity you express, the greater the level of your audience's understanding. If you are unclear about your purpose, your writing will not make a strong connection with the audience.

*Example 4*
Purposes

*Exercise 6*
For the letter that follows at the end of this exercise, answer the following questions:

- Who is the writer?
- What is her topic?

- What is her thesis: topic, position, and analysis—answer to how or why?

- Who is her primary audience? Her secondary audience?
- Which type of document (text) is it?
- Where does her document appear? When? (context)
- Why is she writing this document (purpose)?

The letter provided below is found in *Operation Homecoming: Iraq, Afghanistan, and the Home Front, in the Words of U.S. Troops and Their Families*, a collection of correspondence edited by Andrew Carroll, between soldiers and their loved ones in wartime. *Operation Homecoming*. "Personal Narrative, Specialist Kristina 'Ski' Kolodziejski." Reprinted with permission of Kristina "Ski" Kolodziejski. Kristina "Ski" Kolodziejski, about whom Carroll provides the following background information:

Manning a .50-caliber machine gun mounted on top of a Humvee, twenty-one-year-old . . . Kolodziejski regularly patrolled the streets of Baghdad with the 617th Military Police Company (attached to the 18th Military Police Brigade) during a one-year deployment to Iraq. Kolodziejski was a member of the U.S. Army National Guard out of Kentucky and was called up in the fall of 2004. In February, 2005, while driving through the eastern outskirts of Baghdad, Kolodziejski watched as a group of young Iraqis converged excitedly on a small convoy of American vehicles in hopes of getting candy. Kolodziejski's attention quickly turned to one child who was standing at a distance from the rambunctious crowd. What happened next prompted Kolodziejski to write a short account after returning to base. (112–113)

**Table 1.6  Purposes**

| Central: | Other examples (could be categorized under "Central" purposes): | | |
|---|---|---|---|
| To explain | To agree | To disagree | To inspire |
| To narrate | To blame | To entertain | To motivate |
| To persuade | To call to action | To eulogize | To praise |
| To analyze | To convey feelings | To express opinions | To vent |

Specialist Kolodziejski wrote this personal narrative (the letter referred to above) on February 2, 2005:

I remember pulling over on the side of the road in our squad's three Hummers. We were conducting a security halt to get out and stretch before continuing on with patrolling the routes. The sky was partly cloudy, and the weather was warm, the way springtime feels at home in the United States.

School must have just ended because a large number of Iraqi children were outside and then began approaching our vehicles to receive some free candy, which we often gave out to the kids. Some of them seemed just plain greedy, screaming, pushing, and swarming the vehicles like ducks feeding frantically on thrown bread crumbs.

A small girl of no more than eight or nine years stood by herself in the rear of the wild youngsters, watching her peers scoop up all of the treats being handed out. She timidly folded her arms across her chest and observed quietly.

We finally made eye contact. As she was looking at me, I pointed to the blonde hair pulled up into a small bun in the back of my head, trying to make her realize that I too was a girl. A smile suddenly came to her face. In that moment I remembered that females of this culture do not have the freedoms that we American women possess.

Once the noisy group of mostly boys descended on another truck, I watched as the small girl moved shyly toward me. I leaned down and smiled brightly at this beautiful child with dark hair and dark skin. I handed her a full bag of candy, a gift of gold to the girl, and she seemed overjoyed. The young child gazed at me appreciatively for a moment and then very politely said, "Thank you" in English. I nodded my head and replied, "Shukran," which is "thank you" in her language. Whether or not I made a real difference in that small girl's life I can't say for certain, but I know for a fact that she made one in mine.

*Chapter 2*

# Forming an Argument

## *Aristotle's Parts of an Argument*

### ESSENTIALS

*Note*: As we discussed in chapter 1, Aristotle's classical model for argumentation continues to inspire modern writers and speakers.

*How does a writer form an argument?* Each part of Aristotle's classical model of argument builds upon previous parts to increase the persuasiveness of the argument that is being advanced. Aristotle's model for oration (speeches) in Ancient Greece consists of six parts: Exordium, Narratio, Partitio, Confirmatio, Refutatio, and Peroratio. This model should apply to writing assignments in different courses; however, required formats will vary depending upon the discipline. The main point is that an ancient method of persuasion is still used in argumentative papers in modern courses.

*What is the central purpose of many college writing assignments?* Research, in support of conclusions. This research may be primary—experiments, interviews, or the introspection required in philosophy and religious studies courses—or secondary— printed and electronic texts. College writing classes generally require research papers or researched arguments as practice for the varied assignments you will encounter in humanities, social science, and science courses.

*What can the classical model of argument provide for your research papers?* This model provides a framework for your research paper as well as a strategy for analyzing the texts that will furnish your supporting evidence. Following the strategies presented here will transform your research paper from a formulaic exercise to a thoughtful argument that might move a real audience to action.

The classical model outlined below shows common information in each part of Aristotle's Argument. This model is useful for persuasive research papers in such courses as English, history, or humanities, or social science.

### CLASSICAL MODEL

1. Exordium (Introduction)
   - Creative opening: Example, quotation, surprising fact, or question
   - Exigence: Need, problem, or urgency
   - Background information: What is at issue? What does my audience already know about my topic? What does my audience need or want to know about my topic? What information do I need to refresh for my audience? Transition sentence(s) to thesis; hint at the side of issue on which you stand
   - Thesis statement
2. *Narratio* (Narration)
   - History of topic—extent depends on audience's familiarity with topic
3. *Partitio* (Partition)
   - Establishes points to be proven in *confirmatio*; serves as a preview of subtopics
   - Some classical models use *partitio* as the thesis statement
   - (Shortest part of argument)
4. *Confirmatio* (Confirmation)
   - Evidence: point-by-point proof of thesis statement
   - (Longest part of argument)

5. *Reformatio* (Rebuttal)
   - Counterargument
   - Establish
   - Explain
   - Exploit
   - Note: See Instructors Guide, chapter 2, for information on "Writing a Rebuttal (*Refutatio*)."
6. *Peroratio* (Conclusion)
   - Restatement of thesis with creative repetition
   - Partition of main points
   - Clincher sentence: philosophical statement about topic

## STASES: CATEGORIES OF ARGUMENT

*What are the main categories of arguments?* (1) qualitative, and (2) quantitative.

*What are qualitative arguments?* Descriptive arguments that tell a story; arguments which involve prescribing a certain *action*, which propose causes and effects, which involve *comparison* and *contrast*, which *define* issues, which provide *examples*, which *evaluate*, which describe existing realities (questions related to *existence*), which pays respect to *tradition*, which convey *values*—are all examples of qualitative arguments.

*What are quantitative arguments?* Numerical or statistical arguments that tell a story about the data or information.

*What is a stasis?* Another name for a category of argument. A way of thinking about the heart of an argument. A series of key questions associated with each category that address what is at issue in an argument. By placing your topic into each category, you begin to look at all sides of the issue. The Ancient Greeks used the word "stasis," which translates to "stand," that is, where they stood physically to best connect with their audiences. By choosing a stasis, you too are taking a stand or position on an issue in the process of writing an argument. Choose stasis that best fits your stand on the topic.

*How are stases beneficial to you, a writer?* To narrow research process and form an argument framed appropriately for primary audience.

*How do stases work together?* They can be placed on a metaphorical ladder, whose lower rungs contain lower-level agreements and whose higher rungs contain higher-level agreements. For instance, two opponents must first agree that a problem exists, then define and state facts of the problem; next, they must propose actions to solve the problem; and last, they must vote on an effective course of action which reflects common values of both sides.

Example 1

- *Action*: The Board of Education should move school starting time from 7:45 a.m. to 8:30 a.m.
- *Causality (Cause/Effect):* Since high school students are chronically tired, they are not attentive in class, and their academic performance suffers.
- *Comparison/Contrast*: In 2014, Holland High School moved its starting time from 7:45 a.m. to 8:35 a.m. with successful results in students' attitudes and attentiveness. Students at Spartan High School begin classes at 7:50 a.m., and they appear more tired and less attentive.
- *Definition*: The definition of sleep deprivation is a prolonged period without adequate sleep.
- *Example*: Carlos, a student at Holland High School, feels more alert in his classes, including in his first period of the day—chemistry.
- *Evaluation*: A later starting time is an effective measure of students' academic performance and energy in classes.
- *Existence*: Currently, students are achieving below-average scores on class exams as a result of sleep deprivation.
- *Tradition*: In the history of the school district, starting times have been early. The School Board should set a new precedent and follow the American Academy of Pediatrics' recommendation for later starting times.
- *Values*: Parents, teachers, and students who value academic performance, standardized test scores may be the best advocates for later start times.

### Example of a Quantitative Stasis

*Quantitative*: Of the 860 students enrolled at Spartan High School, 590 voted to push back the starting time of their school day.

### *Exercise 1*
For the following topics, choose the best fitting stases (from Exercise 2 on next page) and explain your choice.

- Concussions in local or national football players
- Internet regulation by government
- Fast food and childhood obesity
- Wind energy

**Table 2.1 Qualitative and Quantitative Arguments**

| Category of Argument: Quantitative | Key Questions | Approach to Argument |
|---|---|---|
| Numerical | How much? How many? How few? | There are _____ of _____, which demonstrates _____. |

### Exercise 2

Find examples of qualitative arguments from an American news site (e.g., CNN, MSNBC, Fox) and a British news site (e.g., BBC)—or any other English-speaking country. Scan the headlines and the articles. Determine which headlines reflect which stases.

Headline from Other Country's News Questions Implicit in Headlines

- Action
- Causality
- Definition
- Evaluation
- Existence
- Tradition
- Values

1. Conduct a miniquantitative analysis, that is, a frequency count of stases as represented by each headline.
2. Which subcategory seems to dominate the American site? And which dominate the other country's site? What comparisons/contrasts can you draw about the two sites?

### Exercise 3

Which stases are represented in these examples?

- Bridges, roads, waterways: What should the state governments do about infrastructure in their cities?
- Bullying laws: Should the state or federal government put laws into place to prevent bullying?
- Cell phones: How have they changed adolescents socially?
- College athletes: Should college athletes be paid?
- Cybercrime: What are the latest ways to steal identity and money?
- Food steroids and antibiotics: How is food manufacturing affecting our food?
- Gap Year: Should students in the United States adopt the British custom of taking a "gap year" between high school and college?

To determine what's at issue, use a "whether" statement.

The issue is whether or not

For example, the issue is whether or not state governments should take action about the poor infrastructure in their cities.

For example, cell phones have or have not affected adolescents' social skills.

## EXIGENCY

*What is exigency?* Exigency is "an imperfection marked by urgency; it is a defect, an obstacle, something waiting to be done, a thing which is other than it should be," according to Bitzer's (1968) explanation (6). In other words, an exigency is a *need, problem,* or a matter of *urgency* to which a writer directs the audience's attention.

*How does a writer establish exigency?* By being aware of the audience's needs and through rhetorical appeals. Students need to consider how to "hook" audience members with respect to their topics. Presenting a lack, need, problem, or source of concern invites audience members to care about their topics.

*Why is exigency an important concept in writing?* As a writer, your work begins early in the paper. Once you have caught your audience's attention, you need to provide a reason for your audience members to keep reading your argument. If you show them that there is something to which they should give their attention, they are more likely to understand the benefits of your argument.

### Example 3 Problem

For instance, in a research paper about widespread poverty in the world and potential solutions for ending it, you could cite Anup Shah's article "Causes of Poverty," posted on the website "Global Issues: Social, Political, Economic and Environmental Issues That Affect Us All," on September 28, 2014. Shah states these statistics:

"Almost half the world—over three billion people—live on less than $2.50 a day. One billion children live in poverty (one in two children in the world). A total of 640 million live without adequate shelter, 400 million have no access to safe water,

**Table 2.2   Prewriting Activity**

General Topic:                                                          Narrowed Topic:

Open-ended question to guide research (begins with How? or Why?):

*Qualitative:*

Category of argument (stases) to frame your paper: (Circle one as primary; you may have a secondary one also):

| | | |
|---|---|---|
| Action | Causality (Cause/Effect) | Comparison/Contrast |
| Definition | Example | Evaluation |
| Existence | Tradition | Value(s) |

*Explain how the stasis best fits your topic:*

Full Rhetorical situation:

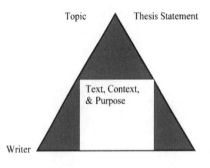

270 million have no access to health services. 10.6 million died in 2003 before they reached the age of five (or roughly 29,000 children per day)."

By citing these statistics, you raise the exigency of the serious problem of poverty. Your audience is likely to take notice as no one wants poverty to exist. Statistics, especially those from a primary source, are an important way to capture audience's attention and set the tone for your paper.

### Example 4 Lack

"Sleep Deprivation in Adolescents and Adults: Change in Affect." *Emotion.* Vol. 10 Talbot, et al., no. 6 (2010):

831–841. Dec., 2010. Talbot, et al.

This article points out the lack of studies on the impact of sleep deprivation in adolescents on specific emotions.

Previous research has tended to examine affect broadly, with little attention paid to the impact on specific, discreet emotions. The affective consequences in *adolescence*, and particularly across development in adolescence, have not been extensively examined. The dearth of experimental research is a critical gap.

By citing these facts, you are establishing a "lack" of studies regarding a topic that is of high interest

for teachers and parents (your audience) who seek more information on the emotional effects of sleep deprivation on their students and children.

### Example 5 Need

In the article "What's Lost as Handwriting Fades" by Maria Konnikova, published on June 2, 2014, the exigency is a need to reconsider the diminishing practice of cursive writing. She writes:

Does handwriting matter? Not very much, according to many educators. The Common Core standards, which have been adopted in most states, call for teaching legible writing, but only in kindergarten and first grade. After that, the emphasis quickly shifts to proficiency on the keyboard. But psychologists and neuroscientists say it is far too soon to declare handwriting a relic of the past. New evidence suggests that the links between handwriting and broader educational development run deep. Children not only learn to read more quickly when they first learn to write by hand, but they also remain better able to generate ideas and retain information. In other words, it is not just what we write that matters—but how.

She quotes Stanislas Dehaene, a psychologist at the Collège de France in Paris, as saying, "When we write, a unique neural circuit is automatically activated." He adds: "This circuit is contributing in unique ways we didn't realize. . . . Learning is made easier."

By citing this fact, you point out the need to reconsider the diminishing practice of handwriting. An audience of young and older adults will likely "tune in" because they learned handwriting in school. They will be interested in lingering benefits from this practice, which may evoke in them memories of their younger days.

*See Appendix for another example of exigency in a college freshman student's paper on the subject of single-sex education.

### Exercise 5

Identify the exigency (need, problem, or urgency) in the opening paragraph of this article: "A Note to Young Immigrants" by Mitali Perkins.

> Be ready: You lose a lot once you're tossed into the mainstream. You lose a place that feels like home, a community where the basics are understood, where conversation can begin at a deeper level. No easy havens await you, no places to slip into with a sigh of relief, saying: "At last, a place where everybody is like me." In the neighborhood, you're like a pinch of chili tossed into a creamy pot. You lose the sharpness of your ethnic flavor quickly but find that you can never fully dissolve. (1)

### Exercise 6

Complete the Invention Worksheet as a prewriting exercise to form your argument.
Audiences:

Primary (Whom do you want to influence responsibly?)

Secondary (Others whom you want to influence?) (Instructor/peers serve as this audience?)

Primary audience characteristics (Which ones are relevant to your audience?):

Based on your selected characteristics, how can you narrow primary audience (ex. Young professionals between ages twenty-two and thirty in the Southeast region who value social justice).

- Thesis statement: Using TAP approach, Topic? Analysis (How? or Why?) Position? Thesis should also reflect the stasis you've chosen. Ex. The state government of Colorado should increase funding for bicycle lanes within the city limits to improve safety of both drivers and riders. *Stasis: Argument by Action
    Rough Draft of Thesis:
    Polished Draft of Thesis:
- Text: Which type of document are you writing?
- Context: Where will you submit your writing: online and/or hardcopy? When is your writing assignment due?
- Purpose(s): Why are you writing this argument (to explain, to analyze, to narrate, and/or to persuade)?

Given your purpose, which type of diction is appropriate for your primary audience?
*Quantitative:*

> What type of quantitative information will support your persuasive position? Ex. statistics, percentages, or other numerical data

Credible Sources that support both Qualitative and Quantitative parts of your argument:

# Chapter 3

# Rhetorical Situations

## ESSENTIALS

*What is a rhetorical situation?* All circumstances that surround a piece of writing. Who is the writer? Who are the primary and secondary audiences? What are the topic and thesis statement? When does the writing take place? Where will the writer submit the document? Why is the writer writing this document? How does the writer use a process to craft the document?

*How is the writing process defined?* Writing is a process to produce a product rather than only a product. Very few people can "give birth to writing whole," so to speak. You may "write" in your mind, then spill the words on the screen, or you may prewrite using an outline or web, or you may simply begin thinking about a topic and write simultaneously. There is no absolute way to approach writing, but each piece of writing benefits from a process of drafting, redrafting, and polishing.

*What are the processes involved in writing?* A late addition to rhetorical theory, the writing process has been promoted in composition classes since the late 1980s. The process has various phases: prewriting, writing, rewriting, and polishing. You may hear different terms for the phases, but all writing processes begin with ideas and end with editing. Though writing is generally a linear process, you may find that it constitutes a recursive system—you may have to revisit stages "out-of-order"—this speaks to the fact that the writing process cannot be described using a list of steps. The central point is to engage in a process that works for you—drafting and redrafting are common experiences that lead to more thoughtful, stronger writing.

*When is the writing process completed?* Many great writers agree that writing is never completed, only abandoned. Deadlines—whether set by yourself, instructor, editor, or any other person invested in the product—may force you to abandon the work perhaps with an unsatisfactory draft. Ideally, however, develop your piece of writing consistently over a period of time; think through your topic fully, and produce a paper that will send the appropriate message to the right audience.

### Example 1
The writing process:

- *Prewriting* (Planning): Generating ideas and giving shape to those ideas
- *Writing* (Composing): Writing a rough draft; focusing on content
- *Rewriting* (Revising): Reworking, transforming, adjusting, and developing content of draft
- *Polishing* (Editing): Correcting conventions (grammar, punctuation, syntax, citations, bibliography, format, pagination, and other surface-level issues)

## WRITING PROCESS CHECKLIST

*Prewriting (Planning)*

1. Understand the rhetorical situation (topic, thesis, primary and secondary audience, purpose, and context) of assignment.
2. Select topic that ignites your interest and begin preliminary research.
3. Form a guiding question that you seek to answer in your thesis statement and writing.

4. Generate ideas about the topic by asking: who? what? when? where? why? On which question(s) do you want to focus?
5. Try brainstorming, freewriting, listing, or webbing.
6. Limit scope or narrow topic.
7. Write a preliminary thesis statement that answers your guiding question.
8. Decide upon an organizational pattern.
9. Organize ideas into subcategories; create sub-headings for subcategories.
10. Select voice to match the rhetorical situation; consider diction and tone that express your voice.
11. *Writing (Composing).*
12. Write a working title that links to thesis statement.
13. Write an introduction.
14. Write topic sentences for entire essay (cross reference them with thesis for purposes of alignment).
15. Introduce evidence (facts, examples, and explanations) for each topic sentence.
16. Select quotations to paraphrase (and cite) or to cite verbatim to support each topic sentence.
17. Add analysis in major paragraphs that support each topic sentence.
18. Unify each paragraph—singular focus.
19. Ensure each paragraph is coherent; include transitional words/phrases within and across paragraphs.
20. Write concluding sentences.
21. *Rewriting (Revising).*
22. Delete excess words, unnecessary repetition, and unrelated evidence.
23. Add further evidence and analysis to support each topic sentence.
24. Add more effective and relevant quotes/paraphrases as needed.
25. Ensure each quote/paraphrase is introduced and integrated.
26. Rearrange ideas within and across paragraphs as necessary.
27. Rewrite partial or full paragraphs to achieve greater unity.
28. Develop more full, effective introductory and concluding paragraphs.
29. Include more transitional words/phrases and sentences to achieve greater coherence.
30. *Polishing (Editing).*
31. Verify proper format. What is required? Title page, running head, pagination, Works Cited, and so forth.
32. Confirm style for documenting sources (e.g., MLA or APA style).
33. Check for consistent verb tense (e.g., historical present tense, past tense, or other), point of view (first-, second-, or third-person), and voice (expressed through tone and diction).
34. Ensure diction is appropriate level for audience; replace words with relevant synonyms as needed; check readability.
35. Statistics (see chapter 7) for grade level to match audience. If audience are educated adults, grades twelve or higher are appropriate.
36. Do an overall copy-edit for surface- and sentence-level errors. An efficient method is to first choose one error, for example, commas in compound sentences.
37. Review your entire document for such errors.
38. Select another type of error mentioned in your peer's and/or instructor's feedback and repeat the process.
39. When copy-editing falters, the reason is that it is hard to focus on too many errors at once. Take a look at each error separately to catch more of them.
40. Correct any grammatical, punctuation, and spelling errors (read your paper aloud, or ask a friend to read your paper to you).

*Note*: The writing process takes time and patience. It is a good idea to allow several weeks to work through the entire process for a typical academic paper. Obviously, this time would extend for a lengthy paper.

## THESIS STATEMENT

### Essentials

*What is the importance of a thesis statement?* A thesis statement is the steering wheel of the essay; without this central statement, the essay is absent of a guiding instrument. A thesis statement is the central idea which all evidence supports in the essay. Generally found at the end of the first paragraph of an essay, the thesis provides the argument's framework: it informs the audience of what they can expect in the rest of the argument. The thesis should include the topic of the argument, the writer's position on the topic, and the analysis (why or how that position will be held).

*What is the difference between a topic and a thesis statement?* A topic is a brief description of the subject. A thesis statement is a sentence or two that express or make an assertion about the topic.

*What is a useful way to write a thesis statement?* When writing a thesis, begin by writing a preliminary thesis. The working thesis will not be perfect (perfection is a myth, anyway!), but the thesis should capture the main point of your argument. As you develop your argument, your ideas may change slightly; therefore, alter your tentative thesis accordingly. When you have finished writing your argument, you should have a reworked thesis that is carefully worded and communicates clearly and concisely.

*Is there an exception to a thesis at the end of an introduction?* In professional and some academic writing, a thesis may be delayed or implicit.

*What are the different purposes for a thesis statement?* A thesis may have different purposes: to inform, to argue, to explain, or others, but despite the purpose, all thesis statements express a point or make an assertion about a topic.

*Why does a thesis statement take on different forms?* The form of a thesis statement varies according to genre, discipline or field, audience, purpose, and context. In other words, the writer adapts the thesis statement to the rhetorical situation.

*Where does a thesis appear in an argument?* In classical arguments, the thesis appears in the introduction, supported by reasons, then possible refutation, and conclusion. Rhetorically, however, it is not always advantageous to state a thesis early in the argument, especially if there is a resistant audience. This refers to a *delayed thesis* in which you introduce your topic, provide reasons, then make an assertion toward the end of argument. Use a deductive, classical approach for an assenting audience (to different degrees), and an inductive approach for a more averse audience.

*What are synonyms for a thesis statement?*

**Table 3.1    Synonyms for Thesis Statements**

| | |
|---|---|
| • Assertion | • Generalization |
| • Central proposition | • Inference |
| • Claim | • Main point |
| • Evaluation/Judgment | • Proposal |

What is a thesis statement? A thesis statement . . .

• is one or two sentences that express the central idea of an essay. Such an idea will become the foundation for all subsequent evidence.

A thesis statement also

• answers an open-ended, guiding question

(A question that requires a reasoned answer; not a "yes" or "no" question A question that begins with How? Which? What? or Why?)

• appears at end of introductory paragraph(s) or evident on first page of paper
• contains point-of-debate word(s) and can be reasonably argued against
• makes your specific assertion, states your position on a topic
• is not too narrow, not too wide in scope
• previews the main point (and subpoints)
• typically written in third person (unless a narrative or other informal essay)
• written in active voice

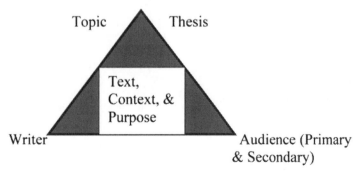

**Figure 3.1    Full Rhetorical Situation.**

*What is not considered a thesis statement?*
A thesis statement does not

- appear as a question or a quotation
- explain only a portion of the argument
- express a vague, unfocused main point
- state a fact that is indefensible
- summarize evidence without making an argument
- (unless a delayed thesis) appear in the middle or end of essay

*What is the goal of a thesis statement?* Take a position (point of view) and influence the audience to not only understand, but to accept a position.

*How do you write a standard or typical thesis statement?*

- Begin with a persuasive topic with more than one side (e.g., school uniforms)
- Research the topic and choose a side: pro or con
- Write an open-ended, guiding question that your thesis statement will ultimately answer.

Examples of Guiding Research Questions
Why are uniforms in middle schools effective in reducing students' behavioral problems? Why is the Atlantic Bridge improvement project exceeding its state budget?

- Turn your question into a thesis statement using the TAP Method.

TAP Method

- T = Topic
- A = Answer to How? or Why?
- P = Position on Topic; Stance an issue (includes point-of-debate word/s)
- In a thesis statement, TAP elements can appear in any order (e.g., APT)

Topic (What? or Who?) + Analysis (Answers the question: How? or Why?) + Position (Stance Thesis Statement)

Example: Arizona middle schools should adopt a uniform policy to reduce student behavioral problems related to the current dress code.

Topic: *Adoption of uniform policy* in Arizona middle schools

Answer to Why? *Reduce student behavioral problems* related to current dress code

Position: Arizona middle schools *should adopt* a uniform policy

a. Weak Thesis Statement: Wind power provides a viable energy source in the Great Plains states. (Topic + Position, but no answer to question: Why? or How?)

***Example 2***

b. Strong Thesis Statement: With potential high winds, vast acreage for wind farms, and a tradition of building windmills for irrigation, the Great Plains states are excellent places for harnessing wind power as a primary energy source. (Answer to question: Why? Topic + Position)
a. Weak Thesis Statement: CFO Wells is a strong leader. (Topic + Position, but no answer to question: Why? or How?)
b. Strong Thesis Statement: [TPA] CFO Wells is a strong leader since she is a concerned, communicative individual who listens well and leads by example. Or [ATP] Since she is a concerned, communicative individual who listens well and leads by example, CFO Wells is a strong leader. (Topic + Answers questions: Who? What? and subordinate clause answers: Why?)

## Point-of-Debate Words

In every thesis statement, there is a point-of-debate word or phrase that expresses your position on the topic. They stress importance, quality, quantity, or magnitude of topic. The point-of-debate word or phrase is the place where people disagree (level of disagreement varies). To discover, complete this sentence:

My primary audience members disagree about
_____ to a(n)
_____ extent.

The key question to discover the point of debate in your thesis statement is this: Where is the place or point in the thesis where someone can disagree with you?

**Examples of Point-of-Debate Words**
many, few, much, multiple, best, better, several, abundant, significant, enough, substantial, sufficient, considerable, particular, effectively, efficiently, consistent, productive, essentially, important, responsive, numerous, safely, exponentially, and more.

*Example 3*

Facebook expanded *exponentially*; therefore, the company became profitable early and now plans upgrades to better accommodate the privacy and usage of its expanding base.

The point-of-debate word is "exponentially" because there is a value judgment involved in word meaning.

a. Vice President Biden is a *substantial* supporter of military members and their loved ones—as shown by his visible presence at bases and family assistance programs.

The point-of-debate word is "substantial" because there is a value judgment involved in the word meaning.

## Absolutes

When writing a thesis, steer clear of "Absolutes" (or statements you believe to be "absolutely true"). Why? You do not appear as fair-minded and open to flexible perspectives to your audience. Also, absolutes are difficult to prove as there are always exceptions to generalizations.

## Continuum of Debate

*Exercise 1*

TAP Method of Analysis

For the following thesis statements, identify the topics, positions, and answers to how or why?

• Genetically engineered food is a threat to human health given the severity of allergic reactions in children.
• Men should receive paternity leave from work since they play a critical role in early natal care and development.
• Several animals raised for food purposes are not slaughtered humanely since slaughterhouses ignore governmental policy.

## Avoiding Absolutes or "Absolutely True" Statements

Improve these thesis statements by converting any absolute words or phrases to more reasonable, fair-minded ones:

1. All adolescents diagnosed with ADHD should eat oatmeal, Greek yogurt, meats, and greens—among other "brain" foods.
2. College athletes should never be paid for their sports performance because they are never members of professional leagues.
3. In the near future, every state needs to legalize medicinal marijuana.

*Exercise 2*

Creating Effective Thesis Statements

Extend these topics to create strong thesis statements: Childhood Obesity, Homeless Veterans, Solar & Wind Power, Racial Profiling

*Exercise 3*

Write guiding questions related to these issues:

Police officers wearing body cameras
Stem-cell research
Motorcycle helmet laws
Price of movie-theater tickets

## TOPIC SENTENCES

*What is a topic sentence?* A statement about the main idea of a paragraph.

**Table 3.3   Potential Topics**

| | |
|---|---|
| • Cell phones and health | • Gun control |
| • Climate change | • Images of women in the media |
| • Drug advertisements to citizens | • Immigration |
| • Drones | • Racial relations |
| • Gap-year for high school graduates | • Social media/academic performance |

**Table 3.2   Continuum of Qualifying Words**

| Absolutely True<br>(All college students are physically fit.)<br>Qualifiers: | Mostly True<br>(Many college students are physically fit.) | Partially True<br>(Few college students are physically fit.) |
|---|---|---|
| all, none, every, any, exact, no one enough, everyone extremely, only complete, tremendous | many, most, multiple better, several, significant, abundant, substantial mainly important, strongly, essentially | few, several, particular, fairly important, insufficient scarce, some, weak, uncommon, or |

This "preview" sentence often includes a comment or analysis point about the topic also.

Topic Sentence: Traveling abroad offers tourists a unique chance to embrace cultures different from their own.

*What is the relationship between topic sentences and a thesis statement?* Topic sentences guide each paragraph, and a thesis guides all supporting paragraphs. For the sake of coherence, topic sentences link directly to the thesis. When both appear on an outline, they should align in meaning. As the thesis statement is the steering wheel of the car, topic sentences are part of the steering system that responds to the driver's participation.

*Where does a topic sentence appear?* Typically, the first or second sentence in a paragraph. The exceptions include (1) a transition paragraph or (2) a "piggy-back"/amplifying paragraph. Since the purposes of these two paragraphs are to connect ideas and to develop an idea further, they do not require standard topic sentences.

*What is the purpose of a topic sentence?* Preview the main idea of the paragraph and set up an expectation for the audience that you will support each part of the topic sentence.

*What is the format of a topic sentence?* Two common formats include

1. Preview: Topic + Analysis (answer to How? or Why?)
   Visiting historical sites such as the Colosseum and the Vatican helps tourists to gain a true sense of history.
2. Review: Topic from previous paragraph & Preview: Topic + Analysis (Answer to How? or Why?) for new paragraph.
   As wonderful as the cuisine may be, there is more to Italy than eating and drinking. Visiting historical sites such as the Colosseum and the Vatican helps tourists to gain a true sense of history.

*What is the point of view of a topic sentence?* It depends upon your writing assignment and its rhetorical situation: purpose, audience, and context. Here are a few diverse examples:

**Text and Point of View**

• Narrative, first person—This morning, because I couldn't find my glasses, I left the house ten minutes later than usual. The day dawned clear, and I got up and stretched lightly.

• Argument, third person—When commuting between city and suburb, many people use public transport, but some prefer to use their own car for the sake of time and efficiency.
• Policy Paper/Memo: First person; third person—In this paper, I plan to discuss three reasons why the school board should fund an expansion of the high-school parking lot to allow student parking spots.

In certain types of writing, there is a place for "meta-discourse," which is an elaborate phrase meaning "about + language." In other words, meta-discourse is telling, rather than showing, readers what you, as a writer, plan to do, then doing your plan, so to speak.

*I will explain the meaning of the term "paradigm,"* which means a system or frame of thinking.
*I believe* people should show their patriotism by visiting historical places in the United States.

Deciding whether to use meta-discourse or not depends on your purpose. As if the information is understood already. If so, delete meta-discourse. For instance, I think the airlines should offer more special discounts for students traveling abroad, the phrase "I think" is understood—therefore unnecessary. The reader knows you think the airlines should offer more special discounts for student travelers or you would not have written this assertion in the first place. The goal is to determine if your instructor expects meta-discourse to appear in an academic paper or other document.

*How do you write effective topic sentences?*
Analysis (Answer to How? or Why?) + Topic
To accommodate its vast number of users worldwide, Facebook revised plans to better protect users from intrusions on their privacy.
or
Topic + Analysis (Answer to How? or Why?)
[Topic] Facebook improved privacy protection [Analysis] following complaints from users.
Topic Sentences for Amplifying Paragraphs
These sentences start major subtopic paragraphs, but rather amplify or "piggy-back" on these paragraphs to provide more evidence.
Facebook is making the "Privacy Checkup" available for its national and international users on their desktops.

***Example 4***
From the collection *War Letters* by editor Andrew Carroll, the following letters are written by soldiers

in World War II and Vietnam wars. War Letter: "Pfc. Edgar Shepard Promises the Parents of Pfc. Russell Whittlesey, Who Saved His Life at Guadalcanal, That He Will 'Avenge' Russell's Death." Reprinted with permission of Andrew Carroll. In a comparison/contrast paper, the writer discussed similarities and differences between the purposes and tones of the letters.

## Background Information

Private First Class (Pfc) Edgar Shepard wrote a letter to the parents of Pfc. Russell Whittlesey, promising them he will "avenge" (197) Russell's Death in the World War II. Russell had saved Shepard's life at Guadalcanal. L. Cpl. (Lance Corporal) Stephen Daniel laments the death of close friend in the Vietnam War in a letter to his parents.

## Sample Thesis

Though separated by decades, Daniel and Shepard wrote letters to express a similar cynicism toward the wars in which they were fighting and to validate the lives of two dead soldiers and friends; they write with fury toward injustice in war and death.

## Sample Topic Sentence 1

Furious at the Marines' callousness toward the death of its soldiers in Vietnam, Daniel seeks to view his soldiers as people; therefore, he particularly validates the life of Corporal Lee Clark, so he and others did not die in vain.

## Sample Topic Sentence 2

Daniel underscores the need to pay respect to fallen soldiers, and Shepard writes a similar sad and angry letter to pay homage to his comrade; Russ then affirms his need to avenge his comrade's death in a search for justice.

### *Example 5*

Here is an excerpt from a recent article (2016) with a sample student thesis and topic sentences about key points of article.

"Social Media and Loneliness: Why an Instagram picture may be worth more than a thousand Twitter Words" by Mathew Pittman and Brandon Reich.

As digital technologies continue to make communication channels and platforms more ubiquitous and effortless, human beings are more connected to each other than ever before. Social media (often referred to as social networking sites, or SNSs) can be broadly defined as the websites and applications that enable users to create and share content with networks (i.e., friends, followers) they construct for themselves. These forms of media have revolutionized how people interact with each other, and young adults are the most avid users. In a recent study, the Pew Research Center found that "fully 91% of smartphone owners ages 18–29 used social networking on their phone at least once over the course of the study period, compared with 55% of those 50 and older" (Smith, 2015, p. 35). Indeed, age is a strong determinant of the frequency and quality of an individual's social media usage, and it is unsurprising that younger people are more comfortable with online communication than adults (Thayer & Ray, 2006 ). In terms of platform popularity among young adults (eighteen to twenty-nine years old) with Internet access, 87 percent use *Facebook*, 53 percent use *Instagram*, and 37 percent use *Twitter* (Duggan, Ellison, Lampe, Lenhart, & Madden, 2015).

Ostensibly, the heightened interpersonal connectivity afforded by social media should be associated with an overall increase in psychological well-being, yet the problem of loneliness persists in the same societies where social media usage is likely at its highest (e.g., the United States, the United Kingdom). According to a nation-wide survey, commissioned by the Mental Health Foundation, 48 percent of British adults believe that people in the United Kingdom are getting lonelier as time progresses, 45 percent report feeling lonely at least some of the time, and 42 percent report having felt depressed due to being alone (Griffin, 2010). Importantly, nearly all indicators of loneliness reported in the survey are of the highest incidence among young adults aged eighteen to thirty-four (as opposed to older adults) (Pittman and Reich 156).

## SAMPLE THESIS

Compared to older adults who use social media less frequently, young adults' frequent social media time is expanding exponentially, yet their sense of isolation is increasing, despite spending more time connecting with peers online.

## Topic Sentence 1

Young adults are using social media platforms: Facebook, Instagram, and Twitter frequently to connect more comfortably with their peers online. [Topic: Social Media Platforms; Analysis: Why? to connect more comfortably with their peers; Position: frequently and more comfortably.]

## Topic Sentence 2

Even though young adults connect with peers on social media platforms frequently, approximately 45 percent experienced increased loneliness due to different quality interactions. [Topic: Young adults connecting with peers; Analysis: Why? different quality interactions; Position: frequently and increased loneliness.]

### *Exercise 4*

Drawing from excerpt below, using your own words, write a thesis that captures key point and takes a position; then write two to three topic sentences that support thesis.]

"Why do college students prefer Facebook, Twitter, or Instagram? Site affordances, tensions between privacy and self-expression, and implications for social capital" by Christina Shane-Simpson, Adriana Manago, Naomi Gaggi, and Kristen Gillespie-Lynch.

"Because some level of online disclosure is necessary to "write oneself into being" on SMSs (boyd, 2008), users must navigate issues of privacy and trust when engaging with SMSs. Tensions between the desire to seek attention from others through online self-expression and privacy concerns, or the degree to which people are concerned that information they post online will spread indiscriminately, have been reported in prior research (e.g., Utz & Kramer, 2009). People may prefer a specific SMS because they feel they can trust the site to support them in negotiating self-expression and privacy online. Feelings of trust may derive from privacy controls available on a given site, the public reputation of the site, and personal privacy concerns. Kwon, Park, and Kim (2014) found that the perceived security of Facebook and Twitter influenced attitudes toward each site; positive attitudes were associated with greater intentions to use each site. Likely due to the flexible privacy settings available on Facebook, but not Twitter, Facebook was perceived as more secure than Twitter. The sense of control that Facebook's privacy settings provide may encourage users to disclose more to their "Facebook friends" over time while using

privacy settings to limit disclosure to "strangers" (Stutzman, Gross, & Acquisti, 2012). Although flexible modifications of privacy settings can be used to direct personal information to select others within one's network, such modifications generally do not reduce the increasingly vast amounts of personal information users are disclosing (perhaps unknowingly) to the corporations running the sites. Consistent with the Marichal (2012) assertion that Facebook has created an "architecture of disclosure," Stutzman et al. (2012) found that over a period of five years, Facebook users employed progressively more sophisticated privacy settings to limit the amount of information available to the general public while sharing increasing amounts of information within their private networks. Perhaps because personal disclosure is often a central aspect of communication on Facebook, perceived security of information was more strongly associated with the intention to use Facebook than Twitter" (Kwon et al., 2014).

Thesis

Topic Sentence 1
Topic Sentence 2
Topic Sentence 3

### *Exercise 5*

Write three topic sentences for one of these topics:

- A way in which Freedom Riders changed racial prejudice
- An approach to learning computer programming for elderly people
- One reason to elect a female president
- One reason why the Internet is censored in China
- One health benefit of eating less-processed food

Try both ways:

Topic + Analysis (Answer to How? or Why?)
Analysis (Answer to How? or Why?) + Topic

## THE PARAGRAPH

### Essentials

*What is a paragraph?* A paragraph is a group of sentences that conveys a main or central idea. A paragraph consists of a clear purpose, a topic sentence, several sentences that support the topic sentence, a concluding sentence that restates the main idea, and, perhaps, previews the next main point.

*What are important features of a paragraph?* Similar to keys on a keyboard, sentences in a paragraph need to cohere or unify to support a central point. All sentences in a paragraph are interrelated, that is, acting in tandem rather than parallel form. Content across sentences often reflects the "Given-New" method discussed in chapter 7. Coherent paragraphs do not wear down the patience of your audience. Instead, they give enough information that "sticks together" and does not place the burden of inference too heavily on the audience.

Each paragraph of every paper or document, for example, narrative, expository paper, research, critical reviews, letter to editor, college-application essay, business letter, or analysis, speaks to the larger purpose of the document or assignment.

*What does a paragraph require?* A paragraph requires (a) unity: singular topic and purpose; all evidence advances and supports a central idea; (b) coherence: all evidence is clearly interrelated to support the topic sentence; and (c) development: enough supporting facts, reasons, examples, and citations to fully develop the central idea.

*How do you achieve coherence in a paragraph?* To achieve coherence, include transitional words and phrases (see chapter 7). Transition means "passage from one place, state, or act to another." Transitions appear in sentences, between sentences, and among paragraphs.

As a "tour guide" of your own writing, use transition words and phrases to connect ideas that point forward and backward. Show the audience the smooth path and help them to pay attention to your most significant points without any burden. The onus of clarity always rests on the shoulders of the writer. The onus of comprehension always rests on the shoulders of the readers. Working together, the writer and reader strive for a "match" between expression and understanding.

*How do you organize details in a paragraph for coherence and effect?* The most common organizational patterns include the following:

- Chronological: Introducing items in the order in which they occurred or in a certain planned order in which they develop

- Order of Importance: Sequencing details from least to most important or from most to least important
- Periodic: Building anticipation until the end of the paragraph
- Spatial: Organizing details into a visual image or scene
- Temporal sequence: Explaining how to create or do something
- Time sequence: Explaining the relationship between ideas/events and the passing of time

*Evidence in Paragraphs*
*How do you develop a paragraph to a satisfactory level for the audience?*

**Table 3.4   Types of Evidence**

| Anecdotes | Definitions | Details | Examples |
|---|---|---|---|
| Explanations | Facts | Illustrations | Numerical Data |
| Paraphrases | Quotes | Reasons | Statistics |

### *Exercise 6*

"Stages of Memory—Encoding Storage and Retrieval" by Saul McLeod. simlypsychology.org. 2007. Web. 22 April 2015.

Memory is essential to all our lives. Without a memory of the past, we cannot operate in the present or think about the future. We would not be able to remember what we did yesterday, what we have done today, or what we plan to do tomorrow. Without memory, we could not learn anything. Memory is involved in processing vast amounts of information. This information takes many different forms, for example, images, sounds, or meaning. For psychologists, the term *memory* covers three important aspects of information processing: encoding, storage, and retrieval. (1)

- Which type of paragraph is shown here?
- Who is the primary audience?
- What is the purpose?
- Which transitional words are present?
- What is the central question(s)?
- What is the organizational pattern of details?
- Which types of evidence are present?
- What are the sentence functions?
- Overall, to what extent does the paragraph achieve its purpose for its audience?

## PARAGRAPHS WITH SPECIFIC FUNCTIONS: INTRODUCTIONS

### Essentials

*What is important to know about writing introductions?* An introduction either engages or disengages an audience. In an essay, proposal, research paper, letter, e-mail, memo, or other persuasive document, the opening creates the first impression, which is often a lasting impression. Therefore, it is important to "hook" your audience so they keep reading and understand your argument.

*Where does an introduction fit into the writing process?* Though our instincts tell us to write an introduction first, then the thesis statement, followed by evidence paragraphs, and finally, the conclusion, writing is a recursive process that is not always linear. In truth, there are no rules against writing an introduction later in the writing process after you have thought about ideas. Another approach is to write a rough draft of an introduction then return to this part later to redraft so that the content aligns more accurately; otherwise, there is a mismatch between an early introduction and later evidence.

*What are different forms of an introduction?* Depending on the rhetorical situation surrounding your writing, an introduction has different forms. There are "standard" or common elements of an introduction in a classical argument called an "Exordium" in most papers and documents that include (1) capture audience's attention, (2) establish a connection or "rapport" with the audience, and (3) state the thesis of the argument.

*Which role does exigency play in an introduction?* As discussed in chapter 2, exigency—a critical concept in any type of nonfiction writing—is a need, problem, or urgency that motivates an audience to care about your topic. Remember that your primary audience listens to a radio station: WIIFM—What's In It For Me? This suggests they are listening for a reason to care about the topic and take any necessary action (spend time, donate money, write a letter to a senator, update a policy, or other). Creating exigency in your papers also serves to capture your secondary audience: instructor and peers—in a positive manner.

*How much background information should you provide for your audience?* So that your audience members keep reading, it is important not to give too little or too much history and background information. Decide which of the journalistic questions: Who? What? When? Where? Why? How? to include and focus only on those parts for sake of efficiency.

*What common elements of an introduction in a classical argument are still appropriate for modern writing?* 1. An attention-grabbing statement (or "hook") to open introduction

- Anecdote
- Fact/Statistic
- Question
- Quotation
- Background context (amount/extent depends on audience's familiarity with topic)
  - What is at issue?
  - What does my audience already know about my topic?
  - What does my audience need or want to know about my topic?
  - What information do I need to refresh for my audience?
- Exigency
- Transition sentence(s) to preview thesis
- Thesis statement

### Example 7
Sample Introductory Paragraph:

"Today around seven-in-ten Americans use social media to connect with one another, engage with news content, share information and entertain themselves. Explore the patterns and trends shaping the social media landscape over the past decade below. When Pew Research Center began tracking social media adoption in 2005, just 5 percent of American adults used at least one of these platforms. By 2011 that share had risen to half of all Americans, and today 72 percent of the public uses some type of social media. As more Americans have adopted social media, the social media user base has also grown more representative of the broader population. Young adults were among the earliest social media adopters and continue to use these sites at high levels, but usage by older adults has increased in recent years." (Pew Research Center, "Social Media Fact Sheet").

### *Example 8*
Sample Introductory Paragraph
  Fighting in Vietnam
  In the midst of cannons shooting and gunshots firing, perhaps the American servicemen tried to recall the words of the National Anthem, reminding

**Table 3.5   Writing Paragraphs**

| Types of Paragraphs | Purpose for Readers (Based on Bloom's Taxonomy) | Transitional Words | Central Questions of Paragraphs |
|---|---|---|---|
| Analysis* AEA method | To analyze | accordingly, for these reasons, furthermore, because, thus | Why is this evidence about_____ significant? |
| Cause/effect | To examine | since, as a result, due to, thus, therefore, consequently | What is the relationship between ____and ____? |
| Classify | To comprehend | in this category, first, second, third;, specifically, here, there | How would you categorize _____? |
| Compare/contrast | To analyze | on the other hand, however, although, but, opposed to, similar to, different from, conversely, while this is true, nevertheless, still, likewise | How does ____ compare or contrast to ____? |
| Conclude | To evaluate | therefore, accordingly, in closing, consequently, thus, as a result, for this reason, in retrospect | Which conclusion can you draw_____? |
| Define | To analyze | which means, defined as, limited to, to explain | What is the meaning of the term_____? What are other ways to explain the meaning of the term? |
| Describe | To gain knowledge | To illustrate, for example, for instance, specifically, in addition, also, furthermore | Who, what, when, where_____? |
| Enumerate | To gain knowledge | first, second, third; before, then, next, finally, eventually, after, following this, last | Which information is placed first, second, third, and so forth? |
| Evaluate | To evaluate | to conclude, in brief, thus, consequently, accordingly, as a result, therefore | Which criteria would you use to assess _____? |
| Explain | To comprehend | for example, for instance, such as, in this case, to illustrate, to demonstrate, simply stated | What is the main idea of_____? |
| Expound | To analyze | Moreover, in addition, besides, furthermore, again, also, too, increasingly, to underscore | What is further information to support the topic_____? |
| Illustrate | To apply | For instance, for example, to illustrate, as an illustration | How can you paint a picture with words to express_____? |
| Inform | To understand | additionally, in addition, in brief, indeed, that is, for example, and then, equally important, next, on the whole | What is the central idea of _____? |
| Narrate | To comprehend | to demonstrate, then, presently, in those days, thereafter, now, later, after that | What happened during a certain period of time_____? |
| Problem or Solution | To apply | in this case, therefore, thus, to introduce, in fact, for example | Which changes would you make to solve_____? |
| Persuade | To synthesize | specifically, to consider, for instance, for example, to illustrate, for these reasons, because, previously, next, still | What might happen if you combined ____with ____? What are your key arguments about_____? |
| Refute | To analyze | however, and yet, but, on the other hand, conversely, in contrast, although this is true | What is the strongest counter-argument_____? |
| Summarize | To comprehend | In brief, to conclude, summing up, overall, for these reasons | What is the main point of_____? What are the subpoints of_____? |
| Trace | To gain knowledge | first, second, third; at length, soon, afterwards, finally, then, previously, formerly, next, thereafter, presently, eventually | What can you learn by recreating the steps of _____process or event? |

themselves of their purpose for fighting in the ongoing, raging Vietnam War. When Americans entered the Vietnam War in the 1960s, the war was surrounded with controversy by military officials, government leaders, and civilians alike. For those one-half million military members who served in the war, there was a high psychological price to pay for their involvement in war when the goal of preventing the spread of Communism proved difficult to achieve. The public had mixed feelings toward the servicemen who embodied the brutalities of the battle. As a result of the Vietnam War, the veterans have suffered social and psychological difficulties for which they need more intensive treatments.

## *Exercise 7*

• Label parts of an introductory paragraph: attention-grabbing statement (hook), background/context, exigency, transition sentence to preview thesis, and thesis statement.

"The Power of Birth Order" by Linda DiProperzio

Each time Elizabeth Moore returns from the supermarket, she expects her sons to help her unload groceries from the car. Her oldest, 13-year-old Jake, is always the first to help, while her youngest, 8-year-old Sam, complains the whole time. Meanwhile, her middle son, 10-year-old Ben, rarely makes it out of the house. "He gets held up looking for his shoes. By the time they've turned up, we're done," says the West Caldwell, New Jersey, mom. "It amazes me how different my children are from one another."

How do three kids with the same parents, living in the same house, develop such distinct personalities? A key reason seems to be birth order. Many experts believe that a child's place in the family is intertwined with the hobbies he chooses, the grades he'll earn in school, and how much money he'll make as an adult. "For siblings, the differences in many aspects of personality are about as great as they would be between a brother and a sister," says Frank Sulloway, PhD, author of *Born to Rebel: Birth Order, Family Dynamics, and Creative Lives*. Birth order isn't the only factor that contributes to how a kid turns out, but giving it consideration can help you understand your kids' personalities—so you can help them succeed in their own unique ways.

## *Exercise 8*

For an upcoming assignment, answer these questions for an effective introductory paragraph:

1. What is the rhetorical situation to which your argument responds?
2. What are the central issues in my argument? What position am I taking on this issue?
3. What is the best way to capture and focus my primary audience's attention early in the argument?
4. How can I establish my credibility (also called intrinsic ethos)?
5. What is the most important point(s) to make about my topic that link to the title and subsequent topic sentences?

## *Exercise 9*

How do you decide which technique: anecdote, fact/statistic, question, or quotation, to open your paper? This depends on your rhetorical situation: topic, audience, purpose, context, and text. For instance, if your essay is about hybrid cars, you may start with a surprising statistic about the growing number of these cars in America to persuade car buyers in a persuasive argument to consider an alternative type of car.

In the following, create rhetorical situations related to the sample topic. Next, create an opening sentence related to the type of hook presented.

Rhetorical Situation

a. Audience: b. Purpose: c. Text:
Topic: Privacy and the Internet
Hook: Anecdote

---

Rhetorical Situation:
a. Audience: b. Purpose: c. Text:
Topic: Effective treatment for depression
Hook: Fact/Statistic

---

Rhetorical Situation
a. Audience: b. Purpose: c. Text:
Topic: Climate change/global warming
Hook: Question

---

Rhetorical Situation
a. Audience: b. Purpose: c. Text:
Topic: Effects on music industry from citizens digital downloading songs.
Hook: Quotation

---

## PARAGRAPHS WITH SPECIFIC FUNCTIONS: CONCLUSIONS

### Essentials

*Why are conclusions a significant part of arguments?* Readers tend to "remember best what they read last," and conclusions leave a lasting impression. Writers create arguments that they believe have value and are worthy of consideration by readers. Accordingly, writers have delivered assertively and carefully. Conclusions also give writers a chance to reiterate a point and say something related to the "bigger picture" or scope of the topic.

*What are the real purposes of conclusions?* A conclusion should prompt your readers to act upon, reflect on, or affect change on an issue. Conclusions serve to call readers to action, whether telling a cautionary tale, foreshadowing what is possible if action takes place, or describing the benefits of action, or other. The call to action should inspire readers to bring about change.

*Why are conclusions challenging to write?* A conclusion is often overlooked or underwritten part of an essay, report, or other document. Sometimes it seems conclusions are tacked on or reflect the loss of steam. Sometimes, writers feel as though there is nothing left to say. Sometimes, conclusions are written repetitively and fall short.

* "Peroratio" in Aristotle's Parts of an Argument
*What are the makings of an effective conclusion?*

1. Plan the conclusion from the beginning. When prewriting/selecting/arranging, think of how you will conclude. Consider the flow of an essay not as linear—but as circular. Bring the audience back to the starting point. Most of the techniques of writing introductions contain within them the ideas of the conclusions—if only the writer will think before writing.
2. Focus on the given (rather than new) ideas. Reflect on content of the essay, rather than beginning anew. If a great new idea occurs to you after you have written the paper, either rewrite the essay or save idea for another writing assignment.
3. Use mirror strategy to write conclusion that mimics form for introduction: hook, exigency, background, transition, and significant statement.
4. Signal the end of the essay. Indicate to the reader that the discussion is now coming to a close.

5. Offer a sense of completeness. A conclusion should not merely restate what you've already said, or belabor the obvious. (Resist the urge to cut-and-paste your introduction or topic sentences.) The most ineffective conclusions are the ones that say this: "In summing up my conclusions, I hope I have proven my point by telling you A, B, and C [in exactly the same language as before, too]. I hope you have liked my paper." Do NOT merely stop because you have run out of things to say. Do not "apologize" for any weakness in your work—real or imagined.
6. Leave a lasting impression on the audience. The conclusion should emphasize the writer's viewpoint or otherwise central impression which the essay has created for the audience.

Reenvision your primary audience, purpose, and context. Which information to refresh to leave a lasting impression?

*What are different types of conclusions for persuasive academic writing?*
Deductive (General to Specific)

- Restating thesis using creative repetition
- Reestablish answer to question: What's at Issue?
- Draw particular conclusion based on evidence
- Synthesis
- Connect various pieces of evidence from several articles or subtopics

Inductive (Specific to General)

- Restating purpose and main details
- Drawing an inference from evidence

*Opening*

- Address the guiding question(s) which started your argument
- Reference to the hook of your introduction
- Restate your thesis using creative repetition (different words, same meaning)

*Content (Options)*

- Answer questions: What do you want your audience to DO? accept your point of view? take action?
- Interpret or evaluate your evidence

- Introduce a relevant quote (reinforces points rather than introduces new information)
- Offer insight from your research (What did you learn that is helpful for audience to know?)
- Point to broader implications or impact of topic on other research, trends, or fields
- Present findings from your research
- Propose a course of action, a solution to an issue, or questions for further study
- Provide a summary and/or synthesis of your argument (Which one? or both?)

*Closing*

- Include a clincher statement—closing sentence as your last word on the subject
- Look to the future—what is next for the research?
- End in a meaningful way so your audience leaves feeling satisfied with your argument

If your conclusion paragraph becomes lengthy, break your paragraphs into penultimate ("second to last") and final paragraphs. In your penultimate paragraph, include a summary and/or synthesis while answering your guiding question.

### Example 9
Freshman College Student's Composition Paper Cara's rhetorical analysis of Franklin D. Roosevelt's "First Presidential Inauguration" Address in March 1933, Persuasive, Deductive Conclusion:

By using his honesty and logic, the newly sworn-in President Roosevelt was able to win over the faith of the American public during this dire time. His assertion that he would not hesitate from assuming "broad Executive power to wage a war against the emergency" (Roosevelt) was met with the loudest applause of the day, displaying the trust he had gained from the citizens of America. This success can only be attributed to his strong charisma which emanated from his words of assurance, as well as his promise enveloped in a clear and direct plan of action that would revive the American nation. Although these were the two main appeals which persuaded the public to place their trust in their new President, his rhetorical techniques in using simple, clear phrases, repetition, and metaphors reinforced his determination to convince the public that he had the answer to their frustrations. During that time of darkness, the newly sworn-in President Roosevelt stood on Capitol Hill and successfully persuaded the public that America had not failed, and that his plan would return the country to its foundation of practical and enduring strength on which it was built.

### Example 10
Freshman College Student's Composition

Mark's research paper: "Is Cultural Awareness becoming America's Weapon of Choice?" Persuasive, Inductive Conclusion:

In studying the progression of America's use of cultural awareness in military operations, it is clear that it is becoming more and more of a necessity to successful missions. As American soldiers are asked to spend more time occupying and rebuilding diverse regions of the world, the government can only help them by properly training them in cultural awareness. America needs to link its vast anthropological resources with its tremendous military capabilities in order to improve combat success and protect American lives. The shift of a soldier's duties from warrior to translator, diplomat, and nation-builder marks a significant and permanent change in the American military. The only way American soldiers can improve in these endeavors is if the government continues to support their training and encourage their cultural awareness development. Improving the link between diplomacy and military operation, local citizens and American command, and the expansion of Arabic-speaking soldiers are all necessary steps in securing future international peace. This peace will be achieved only if the military invests in arming its soldiers with cultural awareness. Tanks and guns will not win the War on Terror—American soldiers' humility will.

### Exercise 10
For an upcoming writing assignment, answer these questions to form an effective concluding paragraph:

- What is the essence of your thesis?
- What are summary points to connect to your established thesis?
- What insight can you offer about the topic? Step back and assess your own and audience's thinking about the topic.
- How can you close your essay meaningfully?

## ASSERTION, EVIDENCE, AND ANALYSIS (AEA) METHOD

*What is an approach to writing a body paragraph?*
The AEA method is a helpful format for writing

body paragraphs for a persuasive essay. The AEA method is also helpful for understanding other authors' body paragraphs. These paragraphs support your thesis statement or "stand alone" as an answer to a shorter prompt.

*What is the AEA method?* A = Assertion (Claim); E = Evidence; A = Analysis

*What is an explanation of each part of the AEA method?*

*Assertion:* A claim about the nonfiction literature that serves as a topic sentence. An assertion is a statement that conveys your interpretation about the nonfiction piece of literature. An assertion requires proof using clear, relevant evidence.

*Evidence:* Proof that supports the assertion. Evidence includes the following: Context, Example, Explanation, Quote, and/or Paraphrase.

*Analysis:* Explains how or why the evidence is significant or important to the assertion. Analysis shows how the evidence used proves the claim, or supports your thesis or topic sentence.

*Which part of AEA is generally the most challenging to write?* The analysis section often poses more challenges than the assertion and evidence sections. Analysis requires higher-level thinking and asks you to pause and reflect on why or how the information is important. This is where you reflect on the evidence and answer your audience's question: "So what?" The analysis section also reveals your voice as a writer. It is your turn to show what matters in the supporting paragraphs.

*What are examples of openers to analysis paragraphs?*

This shows . . .
Demonstrating . . .
Each one exhibits . . .

### Example 11

James J. DiNicolantonio and Sean C. Lucandec. "Sugar Season. It's Everywhere, and Addictive" *The New York Times*, Op-Ed. Web. 15 February 2015. December 22, 2014.

[*Assertion*] Sugar stimulates brain pathways just as an opioid would, and sugar has been found to be habit-forming in people. Cravings induced by sugar are comparable to those induced by addictive drugs like cocaine and nicotine. And although other food components may also be pleasurable, sugar may be

uniquely addictive in the food world. For instance, functional M.R.I. tests involving milkshakes demonstrate that it's the sugar, not the fat that people crave. Sugar is added to foods by an industry whose goal is to engineer products to be as irresistible and addictive as possible. [*Evidence*] How can we kick this habit? One route is to make foods and drinks with added sugar more expensive, through higher taxes. Another would be to remove sugar-sweetened beverages from places like schools and hospitals or to regulate sugar-added products just as we do alcohol and tobacco, for instance, by putting restrictions on advertising and by slapping on warning labels.

[*Analysis*] But as we suggested in two academic papers, one on salt and sugar in the journal *Open Heart* and the other on sugar and calories in *Public Health Nutrition*, focusing narrowly on added sugar could have unintended consequences. It could prompt the food industry to inject something equally or more harmful into processed foods, as an alternative.

A better approach to sugar rehab is to promote the consumption of whole, natural foods. Substituting whole foods for sweet industrial concoctions may be a hard sell, but in the face of an industry that is exploiting our biological nature to keep us addicted, it may be the best solution for those who need that sugar fix. (DiNicolantonio and Lucandec)

### Example 12

Excerpt from: David Elkind, a professor Emeritus of Child Development at Tufts University, in his March 2010, *The New York Times* article: "Playtime is Over."

Now that most children no longer participate in this free-form experience—play dates arranged by parents are no substitute—their peer socialization has suffered. One tangible result of this lack of socialization is the increase in bullying, teasing, and discrimination that we see in all too many of our schools. Bullying has always been with us, but it did not become prevalent enough to catch the attention of researchers in the 1970s, just as TV and [later] computers were moving childhood outdoors . . . While correlation is not necessarily causation, it seems clear that there is a link among the rise of television and computer games, the decline in peer-to-peer socialization and the increase in bullying in our schools. We should recognize what is being lost. (1)

The following paragraph reflects the AEA method; each sentence points to Elkind's argument:

Jane's Paragraph:

[*Assertion*] Since the invention of computers and other technologies, American culture has undergone a massive shift due to the ease of virtual communications and the accessibility of information. However, these new technologies have arrived with unforeseen consequences. [Evidence] Dr. Elkind, a professor of Child Development at Tufts University, argues that technology has decreased child participation in peer socialization and, therefore, increased the occurrence of bullying and discrimination. Elkind addresses parents, teachers, child care providers, and others who supervise today's youth to realize the severity of declining social skills and take action. In his *New York Times* article, Elkind urges, "We should recognize what is being lost" (1). [Analysis] He is correct in his assessment of modern society: the childhood of the twenty-first century is becoming lost in a dangerous blur of limited social exposure and discrimination—with technology to blame.

### Exercise 11
Label each part below: Assertion (Topic Sentence), Evidence (Context, Example, Quote, and/or Paraphrase), and Analysis (Why? or How? evidence relates to topic)

### "Vaping Rises Among Teens" from *NIH News in Health*

A new survey found an alarming rise in the number of American teens who tried vaping last year. The study suggests that vaping may be driving an increase in nicotine use for teens.

In vaping, a battery-powered device called an e-cigarette heats a liquid into a vapor that can be inhaled. The vapor may contain nicotine (the addictive drug in tobacco), flavoring, and other chemicals. E-cigarettes can also be used with marijuana, hash oil, or other substances.

Vaping may pose serious and avoidable health risks. Exposure to nicotine during youth can lead to addiction and cause long-term harm to brain development. The vapor can also contain toxins (including ones that cause cancer) and tiny particles that are harmful when breathed in.

More than 44,000 students took part in the 2018 annual survey of drug, alcohol, and cigarette use in eight, tenth, and twelfth graders. About 37 percent of twelfth graders reported vaping in 2018, compared with 28 percent in 2017. Vaping of each substance that was asked about increased. This includes nicotine, flavored liquids, marijuana, and hash oil.

"Vaping is reversing hard-fought declines in the number of adolescents who use nicotine," says Dr. Richard Miech, who led the study at the University of Michigan. "These results suggest that vaping is leading youth into nicotine use and nicotine addiction, not away from it."

"Teens are clearly attracted to the marketable technology and flavorings seen in vaping devices," explains Dr. Nora D. Volkow, director of NIH's National Institute on Drug Abuse. "However, it is urgent that teens understand the possible effects of vaping on overall health, the development of the teen brain, and the potential for addiction."

# Chapter 4

# Appeals and Fallacies

## ESSENTIALS

*What is a rhetorical appeal?* It is an appeal in written or spoken text aimed at persuading audience members to respond, act, and assent to a point of view.

*What are the types of rhetorical appeals?* Logos, ethos, and pathos, which Aristotle describes as "the means of persuasion: logical argument, the presentation of the speaker's character, and moving the emotions of the audience" (qtd. in Kennedy 25). In summary, logos is good sense, ethos is good character, and pathos is goodwill.

*How do the appeals work separately or together?* In writing, the appeals act separately or together to capture the audience's attention and reinforce their convictions. Typically, one appeal is more prominent in an argument. "A sound, persuasive argument will simultaneously establish a strong intrinsic ethos for the writer, appeal to the audience's emotions or sense of identity or shared values, and present cogent proofs in a logical and coherent manner" (*Engagements with Rhetoric* 107).

*Which appeal(s) should you use?* This depends on the rhetorical situation surrounding your writing. Rhetorical appeals are helpful in persuading your audience. Strive to project an ethos of fair-mindedness, intelligence, good reasoning, and forward-thinking. This will create a favorable impression on your audience and help you to achieve your purpose in a credible way.

## Ethos

*Extrinsic*: An appeal made based on external sources of ethics, character, and credibility. While making an extrinsic ethos appeal, stories, articles, books, presentations, testimonials, sermons, and other texts can be drawn on to underscore "the right thing to do" in a particular context.

*Intrinsic*: An appeal made based on the ethics, character, and credibility of the writer or speaker. This appeal refers to the author's reputation that "lives" with texts, which include publications, institutions, films, and more. Aristotle argued that it is important to establish the goodwill of the writer or speaker to persuade audiences effectively. An example of diminished intrinsic ethos is exhibited in this cartoon:

*What is our basis for trusting writers or speakers?* Our perception of their character influences how believable or convincing we find their arguments. We tend to believe speakers whom we find reasonable, trustworthy, and agreeable. We also understand ethos as a writer's personal or professional experiences.

*Do we trust those who are similar to us?* Some argue that persuasion is most likely when the audience identifies with the speaker or writer. In other words, we tend to identify with writers and speakers whom we perceive as "experts" and whom we find relatable. Literary theorist Kenneth Burke argues, "A speaker persuades an audience by . . . identification of interests to establish rapport between himself and his audience" (191).

## Misuse of Ethos

Misuse of ethos involves authority over evidence. As the saying goes, beauty and fame set their own rules. This applies to the misuse of ethos when people with "name value" emphasize their authority as an equality of merit or virtue for a given product or event. For example, famous musicians or athletes

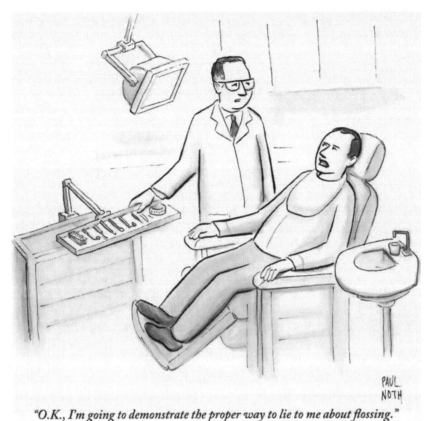

"O.K., I'm going to demonstrate the proper way to lie to me about flossing."

**Figure 4.1  The New Yorker Collection, 2014.** Paul Noth. From cartoonbank.com. All rights reserved.

sell cologne—a product that does not relate directly to their work.

Also known as a status argument, the misuse of ethos in a rhetorical appeal comes from a notion that the greater the authority, the more unquestionable the conclusion or declaration. In a democratic society, no one has unassailable authority; everyone's opinions are subject to scrutiny. It is important to approach persuasive arguments by public or private citizens via an informed rhetorical vaccine, so to speak, and healthy skepticism.

## Pathos

Appeal to emotions. (As an adjective: a "pathetic" appeal.) Stories, humor, sound bites, slogans, and sales techniques are likely to use in pathos-based appeals.

## Logos

Appeal to logic, reasonableness, and rationality. Facts, deductive reasoning, expert testimony, statistics, quotations from texts, and definitions can be used in logos-based appeals. Logos can also include common sense.

## EXAMPLES OF RHETORICAL APPEALS

### *Example 1*

### Ethos

I will end this war in Iraq responsibly, and finish the fight against al Qaeda and the Taliban in Afghanistan. I will rebuild our military to meet future conflicts. But I will also renew the tough, direct diplomacy that can prevent Iran from obtaining nuclear weapons and curb Russian aggression. I will build new partnerships to defeat the threats of the twenty-first century: terrorism and nuclear proliferation; poverty and genocide; climate change and disease. And I will restore our moral standing, so that America is once again that last, best hope for all who are called to the cause of freedom, who long for lives of peace, and who yearn for a better future. (Barack Obama)

I made my mistakes, but in all of my years of public life, I have never profited, never profited from public service—I earned every cent. And in all of my years of public life, I have never obstructed justice. And I think, too, that I could say that in my years of public life, that I welcome this kind of examination, because people have got to know whether or not their president is a crook. Well, I am not a crook. I have earned everything I have got. (Richard Nixon)

## *Example 2*

## Pathos

I am not unmindful that some of you have come here out of great trials and tribulations. Some of you have come fresh from narrow jail cells. And some of you have come from areas where your quest—quest for freedom left you battered by the storms of persecution and staggered by the winds of police brutality. You have been the veterans of creative suffering. Continue to work with the faith that unearned suffering is redemptive. Go back to Mississippi, go back to Alabama, go back to South Carolina, go back to Georgia, go back to Louisiana, go back to the slums and ghettos of our northern cities, knowing that somehow this situation can and will be changed. (Martin Luther King, Jr.)

## *Example 3*

## Logos

However, although private final demand, output, and employment have indeed been growing for more than a year, the pace of that growth recently appears somewhat less vigorous than we expected. Notably, since stabilizing in mid-2009, real household spending in the United States has grown in the range of 1 to 2 percent at annual rates, a relatively modest pace. Households' caution is understandable. Importantly, the painfully slow recovery in the labor market has restrained growth in labor income, raised uncertainty about job security and prospects, and damped confidence. Also, although consumer credit shows some signs of thawing, responses to our Senior Loan Officer Opinion Survey on Bank Lending Practices suggest that lending standards to households generally remain tight. (Ben Bernanke)

## *Example 4*

Sometimes, a sentence, paragraph, and full essays may have primary and secondary appeals. For example, an advertisement for a major car company may stress pride in ownership (primary) while featuring "0%" interest rates for car loans (secondary). The secondary appeals always support the primary appeal as in example below:

## Ethos, Pathos, and Logos

"The perfect amount to leave to your kids, he told *Fortune* [magazine] in 1986, is enough money that they feel they could do anything, but not so much that they could do nothing." (Warren Buffet). His appeals are directed toward audience of parents by using his own family money as an example.

Ethos: Buffet values integrity in both himself and his kids. He stresses to "do the right thing" with inheritances. (Primary Appeal)
Pathos: Buffet conveys value of pride that comes one's own hard work, rather than laziness. (Secondary Appeal)
Logos: Buffet explains his logical approach to leaving inheritance to his kids. (Secondary Appeal)

## *Exercise 1*
In the following quotations, do the speakers make an appeal strongly based on ethos, pathos, or logos? Several quotes reflect primary and secondary appeals.

a) _____ "If we started in 1960, and we said that as productivity goes up, then the minimum wage is going to go up the same. If that were the case, the minimum wage today would be about $22 an hour. . . . So my question is what happened to the other $14.75?" (Elizabeth Warren)
b) _____ "I have reasoned this out of my mind, there was one of two things I had a right to, liberty or death; if I could not have one, I'd have the other" (Harriet Tubman)
c) _____ "I have decided to stick with love. Hate is too great a burden to bear." (MLK, Jr.)
d) _____ "[T]his is the lesson: Never give in. Never give in. Never, never, never, never—in nothing, great or small, large or petty—never give in, except to convictions of honour and good sense. Never yield to force. Never yield to the apparently overwhelming might of the enemy. We stood all alone a year ago, and to many countries it seemed that our

account was closed, we were finished. All this tradition of ours, our songs, our School history, this part of the history of this country, were gone and finished and liquidated. Very different is the mood today. Britain, other nations thought, had drawn a sponge across her slate. But instead our country stood in the gap. There was no flinching and no thought of giving in; and by what seemed almost a miracle to those outside these Islands, though we ourselves never doubted it, we now find ourselves in a position where I say that we can be sure that we have only to persevere to conquer." (Winston Churchill)

e) _____ "Remember no one can make you feel inferior without your consent." (Eleanor Roosevelt)

f) _____ "Love is the irresistible desire to be irresistibly desired." (Mark Twain)

g) _____ "We learned about honesty and integrity—that the truth matters . . . that you don't take shortcuts or play by your own set of rules . . . and success doesn't count unless you earn it fair and square." (Michelle Obama)

h) _____ "Stocks [have] been so much more attractive than bonds." (Warren Buffet)

i) _____ "I am an American, not an Asian-American. My rejection of hypenation has been called race treachery, but it is really a demand that America delivers the promises of its dream to all citizens equally." (Bharati Mukherjee).

j) _____ "Everyone must dream. We dream to give ourselves hope. To stop dreaming—well, that's like saying you can never change your fate. Isn't that true?" (Amy Tan)

### Exercise 2

Examine the following images and determine which rhetorical appeal(s) is (are) most strongly represented in them. When answering the questions, name the appeal(s) and support with textual evidence.

### Logos

• Which factual information, expert opinions, and data have I used to support my thesis statement?

**Figure 4.2   Stop Texts Stop Wrecks Public Service Announcements.**

- Which key terms do I need to define?
- Have I avoided generalizations drawn from data?

### Ethos

- Have I established that I am credible on this topic?
- Have I provided enough evidence for my audience to decide that my argument is credible?
- Have I avoided overstating or understating my points?

### Pathos

- What are the goals of my audience? How do their goals relate to my topic?
- Which values does my audience own? What do they fear? What do they take pride in? What do they sympathize with?
- What is my audience's viewpoint on the topic? Accepting? Unaccepting? Curious? Skeptical?

**Figure 4.3 Public Service Announcement: "Give Your Garbage Another Life: Recycle."** https://www.psacentral.org/home.do.

## LOGICAL FALLACIES

### Essentials

*Where are logical fallacies found?* Persuasive arguments focus on influencing an audience to support a point of view or action. Within the arguments, there are sometimes errors in reasoning or what are known as logical fallacies. They are "logical" because they are strategic, plausible-sounding parts of arguments; however, they depend on faulty reasoning. Speakers and writers use fallacies intentionally or unintentionally. They are common and outwardly convincing, but once examined, they appear feeble, even misleading. You have likely encountered these errors in your daily life—in verbal disagreements, political or other kinds of debates, online discussions, advertisements, in formal and informal publications, and so forth.

*What is important to know about logical fallacies?* As an exercise in "intellectual self-defense" against faulty or fallacious arguments, it is important to understand persuasion (channeling course of events in a given direction) so as to judge the importance or validity of what people say and how they say it. No one has unassailable authority; therefore, everyone's arguments are open to examination to determine if their arguments are valid and lack logical fallacies.

*How are fallacies categorized?* Fallacies are divided according to the rhetorical appeals: ethos, pathos, and logos.

- *Fallacies of ethos* involve the misuse of ethos by misrepresenting authority. For instance, a speaker or author may attempt to present himself or herself as knowledgeable, trustworthy, or interested, when in reality he or she is just trying to take advantage of the audience's trust.
- *Fallacies of logos* involve making arguments that appear rational, fair, and valid, but, in fact, are not sound.
- *Fallacies of pathos* involve emotions that serve an important role in persuasion, especially in moving people to act on their convictions. Fallacies of pathos occur when an author uses emotions to obscure an issue, divert attention away from the real issue, or exaggerate the significance of an issue—all the while appealing to an audience's emotions.

The list of emotions given in table 4.1 is a modern expansion of Aristotle's ancient list.

Example: You may have studied logical fallacies in the past. The examples of arguments that follow contain logical fallacies—you may even spot logical fallacies you have not studied before!

Whether examining or writing arguments, make sure you detect logical fallacies that weaken arguments. Use evidence to support claims and validate information—this will make you appear credible and create trust in the minds of your audience.

**Table 4.1   Aristotle's Expanded List of Emotions**

| | | | | |
|---|---|---|---|---|
| Afraid | Daring | *Indignation | Optimistic | Sympathetic |
| *Angry | Delighted | Infatuated | Overjoyed | Tense |
| Annoyed | Devalued | Intimidated | Overwhelmed | Thoughtful |
| Anxious | Devoted | Irritable | Panicky | Threatened |
| Apathetic | Disappointed | Jealous | Passionate | Thrilled |
| Apologetic | Embarrassed | Jovial | Patient | Tolerant |
| Appreciative | *Emulation | Joyful | Peaceful | Touched |
| Awkward | *Enmity | Judged | *Pity | Uncomfortable |
| Blissful | Enthusiastic | Kind | Pleased | Unkindness |
| Blue | *Envious | Lame | Regretful | Unhappy |
| Bold | Excited | Lively | Relaxed | Upset |
| Bored | Excluded | Lonely | Reluctant | Vengeful |
| Buoyant | *Fearful | Loving | Remorseful | Vibrant |
| *Calmness | *Friendship/Friendly | Melancholy | Resentful | Vindictive |
| Chastened | Furious | Merry | Restless | Warm |
| Cheerful | Grieved | Miserable | Sad | Withdrawn |
| Comfortable | Guilty | Mistreated | Sentimental | Worried |
| Concerned | Happy | Mortified | *Shame/Shame-lessness | Wounded |
| *Confident | Helpless | Neglected | Shocked | Yielding |
| Confused | Hopeful | Offended | Sorrowful | Zapped |

*Aristotle's Original List of Emotions

*Exercise 3*

Determine which logical fallacy is best exemplified in the following statements.

1. _____ Either we require children to exercise several times each week in physical education class, or we watch a firm increase in children who are earning low grades and dropping out of school.

2. _____ A lifestyle that does not include exercise must cause diabetes because a higher percentage of people who do not exercise are diagnosed with diabetes than active people.

3. _____ Exercising irregularly does not lead to a shorter lifespan because my grandmother did not exercise, and she lived until 86.

4. _____ The National Institute of Health (N.I.H.) has an obligation to provide free exercise opportunities for everyone because people without access to gyms have a right to resources provided by the government.

5. _____ If the United States does not adopt the socialist medical plan, more citizens will move to Canada so that they can afford health care for their families.

6. _____ If people do not exercise regularly and get enough sleep, they will risk dying prematurely.

7. _____ Everyone in the neighborhood is joining the local gym, "Get Fit Today!"; therefore, we should also join since our neighbors are losing weight.

8. _____ Mr. Kingston, our physical education teacher, endorses Vitamin D as the most important vitamin an adult should take every day. Look what taking Vitamin D has done for him: greater vitality and he rides his bike to his office.

9. _____ Physical activity helps to reduce body fat by improving the body's ability to burn calories. People who increase their exercise can now eat larger quantities of food.

10. _____ Since several people have become injured while rollerblading in the park, we should ban the sport in the local area.

*Exercise 4*

Peer Exercise

Choose a topic related to your research for a paper, and create five examples of various logical fallacies related to your topic. Exchange with a peer and fill in answers to each other's exercises.

## RHETORICAL ANALYSIS EXERCISE

Analyze Mitali Perkins' article: "A Note to Young Immigrants" and write a rhetorical analysis. Article: "A Note to Young Immigrants" by Mitali Perkins. © Mitali, Perkins. "A Note to Immigrants," *Teaching Tolerance Magazine* 28, Fall 2005. www.tolerance .org.*Appears in full, student text; referred to in Instructors Guide. "A Note to Young Immigrants" by Mitali Perkins

Be ready: You lose a lot once you're tossed into the mainstream. You lose a place that feels like home, a community where the basics are understood, where conversations can begin at a deeper level. No easy havens await you, no places to slip into with a sigh of relief, saying, "At last, a place where everybody is like me." In the neighborhood, you're like a pinch of chili tossed into a creamy pot. You lose the sharpness of your ethnic flavor quickly but find that you can never fully dissolve.

You lose the ability to forget about race. You're aware of it everywhere in town, like a woman aware of her gender in a roomful of men. You dodge stereotypes at school by underperforming or overachieving. You wonder if you're invisible to the opposite sex because you're foreign or because you're unattractive.

You lose a language. You still speak your parents' language, but it will soon begin to feel foreign to lips, pen, and mind. Your heart won't forget as quickly; it will reserve a space for this mother tongue, your instructor of emotion, whispered in love and hurled in anger. Your heart language will speak words that tremble through tears; it will join you with others in the camaraderie of uncontrollable laughter. In your new language, English, you enjoy the lyrical cadence of poetry and glimpse the depth of ancient epics, but your heart will remain insatiable.

You lose the advantage of parents who can interpret the secrets of society. Your friends learn the art of conversation, the habits of mealtimes, the nuances of relationships, even the basics of bathroom

**Table 4.2 Logical Fallacies**

| Fallacy or Error in Reasoning | Definitions | Examples |
|---|---|---|
| | *Fallacies of Ethos* | |
| Ad Hominem | Latin trans: "To the man"; attack person's character to distract others from issue at hand | Questioning a scientist's research findings based on the fact he or she has accrued a series of outstanding parking tickets. |
| Appeal to False Authority | Assuming claim is fact simply because credible person stated claim though not necessarily true | Birth order must qualify as a scientific theory because hundreds of social scientists endorse birth-order studies. |
| Appeal to Tradition | Assuming that what has existed for lengthy time should continue to exist based on tradition | Supermarkets in this town have always bought produce from local farmers, and there have never been customer complaints. |
| Guilt by Association | Refuting someone's arguments or actions by virtue of someone's choice of friends or associates | "Don't listen to her. She's a Libertarian, so you can't trust her opinions on the topic." |
| Poisoning the Well | Discredit an opposing view in advance; presumed guilty | "Of course, this liar will tell you that he didn't steal my stuff. You can't believe a thief. Go ahead and ask him; he'll deny it." |
| Straw Man | Oversimplifying or overstating an opponent's argument to make it easier to refute | I can't understand anyone wanting to cut the defense budget. Why would anyone want to leave our country defenseless? |
| | *Fallacies of Logos* | |
| Begging the Question | Drawing a conclusion inherent in the question; conclusion without adequate support | "Abortion is wrong because it is murder." "You should exercise because it is good for you." |
| Circular Reasoning | Repeating an argument in different words with same meaning | We should sleep in today because of the snowy weather. Since it is snowing heavily, we should sleep in today. |
| Complex (Loaded) Question | Assumes an implied agreement | "Have you stopped drinking so heavily?" |
| Dicto Simpliciter | Simple explanations applied to more complex situations | Eating blueberries can improve one's memory. Therefore, everyone should try to improve their memories by eating blueberries. "The increasing rate of crime among kids all boils down to too much violence on TV." |
| False Analogy | Misleading or implausible comparison | "People get away with murdering children, but we can't get gay marriage legalized in the state of California" (Miley Cyrus). |
| False Dilemma | Either/or; presents only two alternatives when there could be more than two | "Do you want to finish dinner or go straight to bed?" "Do you want to pay cash or credit for that?" "Would you rather buy whole life insurance or risk leaving your family without any income?" |
| Hasty Generalization | Drawing a conclusion based on insufficient evidence | The region of the country is probably going into a recession because they laid off five people at my office. |
| Loaded Label or Definition | Promoting connotative meaning of words | "Study for the midterm, or you'll fail." |
| Non Sequitur | Latin trans: "Does not follow" | Jacob drives an SUV. He must enjoy kayaking and cycling. |
| *Fallacy or Error in Reasoning* | *Definitions* | *Examples* |
| | *Fallacies of Logos* | |
| Pars Pro Toto | Latin trans: "Part for the whole"; assuming what is true for the part is true for the whole | Since the science project failed, we should not have a school science fair next year. |
| Stacking the Deck | Rejecting or omitting opposing arguments | A drug company advertises only the positive results of experiments on a new drug, suppressing any negative results. A used car dealer stacks the deck when he or she only indicates the positive qualities of a vehicle. |

*(Continued)*

**Table 4.2  Logical Fallacies (*Continued*)**

| Fallacy or Error in Reasoning | Definitions | Examples |
|---|---|---|
| Post Hoc/Ergo Propter Hoc | Latin trans: "After this, therefore because of this"; Inference that because one event follows another, the first event must be the cause of the second one. | A person walks under a ladder, and a bucket of paint falls on his head, so he tells people that walking under a ladder brings bad luck. |
| Slippery Slope | Taking a first step will inevitably cause an undesirable chain of events with negative consequences | Error: Walking under the ladder did not cause the bucket to fall. "If you steal a candy bar, then you will steal toys, then bikes, then cars, and then you'll find yourself on death row." Political extremists use the slippery slope fallacy when they argue that one particular bill, this one Supreme Court nominee, or just a slight increase in taxes will all bring the country to unavoidable disaster. |
| Statistics of Small Numbers | Promoting few favorable statistics and assuming they apply to many situations | My parents smoked all their lives and they never got cancer; therefore, smoking does not cause cancer. |
| Sweeping Generalization | Broad statement misapplied to all persons, places, and things | My accounting degree really prepared me well for law school. Everyone who wants to go to law school should major in accounting. |
| *Fallacies of Pathos* | | |
| Ad Populum | Beliefs and biases of the people; appealing to people's sentiments rather than their logic | Vote for a certain candidate due to her challenges growing up in poverty and ability to understand those in need. |
| Argumentum ex Silentio | Latin trans: Appeal to ignorance; claim not proven true or false | Bigfoot, the Loch Ness monster, and extraterrestrials must really exist because no one has ever proved that they don't. |
| Appeal to Pity, Pride, or Fear | Appeal to sympathy when such feelings are irrelevant to argument and people should decide based on objective, relevant evidence | To a police officer: "I was speeding since I was going to buy tickets to a concert when store opened." |
| Bandwagon | One should believe or do something because everyone else does; to board the bus or train on which everyone is riding; assumes opinion of majority is valid | Most nations have socialized medicine, that is, medical care provided by the government. Therefore, the U.S. should adopt a federally funded health care system rather than put the burden on employers. |
| Red Herring | Trans: using an odorous fish to throw dogs off trail; attempt to raise an unrelated or irrelevant point | "I don't think the president's economic plan is a good idea. I mean, what is he going to do about the violence in our inner cities?" |

behavior, from their parents. Your own parents' social etiquette sometimes leads to confusion or embarrassment in the outside world. You begin to take on the responsibility of buffering your parents from a culture that is even more foreign to them. You translate this new world's secrets for them.

You lose the stabilizing power of traditions. The year is not punctuated by rituals your grandmother and great grandmother celebrated. Holidays in this new place lack the power to evoke nostalgia and renew childlike wonder. Your parents' feasts of celebration fall on days when you have to go to school.

You lose the chance to disappear into the majority anywhere in your new world. In the new neighborhood, you draw reactions common to minorities—outright racism, patronizing tokenism, enthusiasm from curious culture-seekers. If you travel across the seas to neighborhoods where your parents grew up, you're greeted with curious, appraising stares. You're too tall or too short; you move your arms and hips differently when you walk; you smile too often or not often enough; you employ the confusing nonverbal gestures from another world.

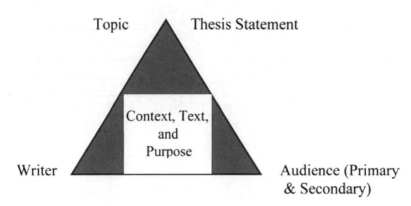

**Figure 4.4  Full Rhetorical Situation.**

But don't get discouraged. In fact, you should feel quite the opposite. There is good news about life in the melting pot. There are gains to offset the losses, if you manage not to melt away altogether. You're boiled down, refined to your own distinctiveness. You realize early that virtues are not the property of one heritage; you discover a self powerful enough to balance the best of many worlds.

A part of you rises above the steamy confusion of diversity to glimpse the common and universal. You recognize the ache that makes us all feel like strangers, even in the middle of comfortable homogeneity. You understand the soul's craving for a real home because yours is never sated with a counterfeit version. So take time to mourn your losses, but remember to revel in the gains. Learn to embrace a litany of genuine labels—words like stranger, pilgrim, sojourner, and wayfarer. Stride past the lure of false destinations, intent on traveling to a place where, at last, everyone can feel at home.

The rhetorical situation:

Author/writer_____
_____

Topic Thesis statement (central message)_____
_____

Primary audience _____ Characteristics of primary audience (age range):
Secondary audience _____
_____

Characteristics _____
_____

Text (Which type of document?) _____
_____
_____

Context (When published? Where published?) _____
_____
_____

Purpose (Why?) _____
_____
_____

Rhetorical considerations:

Category of argument (Stases): Circle one as primary; you may have a secondary one also):
Primary Appeal (Ethos, Pathos, and Logos) _____
_____
_____

Voice_____
_____

**Table 4.3  Audience Characteristics**

| | | |
|---|---|---|
| Age range | Education | Race/ethnicity |
| Background knowledge | Gender | Religious affiliation |
| Beliefs on topic | Geographical location | Socioeconomic class |
| Careers | Interests | Values |

**Table 4.4  Stases: Categories of Argument**

| | | |
|---|---|---|
| Action | Definition | Existence |
| Causality (Cause/Effect) | Example | Tradition |
| Comparison/Contrast | Evaluation | Value(s) |

Larger context:

Exigency(Urgency) _____

_____

Kairos  (Timing) _____

_____

Occasio  (Occasion) _____

_____

_____

Sentence-level strategies:

Diction  (Type?  Level?) _____

_____

_____  Tone_____

_____

_____ Syntax (Sentence style: sim-
ple/complex? periodic/loose? other?)_____

_____

_____

_____

Figures of speech _____

_____

_____

Overall:

Which patterns are present?
How do the patterns relate to the writer's thesis?
What overall conclusion can you draw about Perkins
    fulfilling her purpose for her primary audience?

*Chapter 5*

# Voice

## ESSENTIALS

Note: Voice as used in this chapter is different from the verb forms, active and passive voice, discussed in chapter 7.

*Why is "voice" an important, but sometimes elusive, concept in writing?* Every professional writer has a signature voice. Every writing instructor wants to hear a student's voice. Every student is challenged to express a voice. These statements show that voice is crucial to writing; however, they do not define what is meant by voice. Voice refers to a writer's originality in expression; it is something that he/she discovers as being his/hers rather than something he/she invents or constructs. Your writing instructors may have commented that they want "to hear" your voices in your compositions; however, you may have found this comment abstract, and it may have left you confused about how you are supposed to reveal your voice. You may associate voice with feelings and perspectives and thus with fiction (e.g., a poem or a novel), but voice is also present in nonfiction writing, although in a different way. When attached to words, a writer's voice is heard.

*How is "voice" defined?* For a concept so crucial to writing, it is surprising there are widely varying definitions of "voice." Writers don't seem to agree on a common definition, but they all agree "voice" is a necessary, yet intangible aspect of writing. For the purposes of this text, "voice" is a writer's expression of his/her "self" by disclosing feelings and thoughts. The intensity and extent of this disclosure is determined by the rhetorical situation surrounding the writing.

*When do we use various "voices"?* This depends on purpose, context, and audience. We have something to say, and we decide, often instinctively, which voice to use in which circumstances. For instance, while we may express grief after a pet dies in an e-mail to a friend, in a research paper, we may keep our feelings about stem-cell research to ourselves, preferring instead to just discuss the facts related to the issue. In these and other rhetorical situations, we have different levels of audibility—audibility here does not refer to the volume we turn up on a remote, but rather to the extent to which readers "hear" us in our writing.

*What is voice based upon?* A writer's voice has roots in a longing or desire to say something. What does the writer long to say? To whom? And in which context? To uncover a writer's longing, look carefully at his/her word choices and attitudes toward the topic. In other words, look at the writer's diction and tone. An audience can hear the writer's voice in his/her disclosure of his/her thoughts and feelings about a topic. Here is an important question to ask: To what extent has the writer disclosed his/her feelings and thoughts to express his/her longing?

*How is "voice" expressed in writing?* Through words and through the attitudes expressed toward the subjects being discussed. Voice is expressed through "stylistic devices." A way of thinking about "stylistic devices" is to think of them as features of writing. Examples of stylistic devices include diction (word choice), point of view (first, second, or third person), and tone (writer's attitude toward his/her subject).

Sometimes, the writer's expression is muted; sometimes, his/her expression is confessional to the point where it seems too much is being shared. Most times, however, a writer's expression is somewhere in-between. Voice also ranges between informal and formal, personal and distant.

The places on the continuum are determined by the rhetorical situation.

Informal_____Formal
Personal_____Distant

### Example 1

Walter Isaacson's biography on Steve Jobs, the cofounder of Apple Inc., records the following remarks of Jobs, remarks in which Jobs uses a voice that is formal and direct, in other words a voice that is in-between a voice that is distant and a voice that is personal:

Of Apple products, Jobs argued,

> "We will make them bright and pure and honest about being high-tech, rather than a heavy industrial look of black, black, black, black, like Sony. . . . So that's our approach. Very simple, and we're really shooting for Museum of Modern Art quality. The way we're running the company, the product design, the advertising, it all comes down to this: Let's make it simple. Really simple." (qtd. in Walter Isaacson, *Steve Jobs*. New York: Simon & Schuster, 2011, 126. Print.)

### Example 2

The following is another war letter from Andrew Carroll's book *War Letters*. War Letter: "The Sister of an Army Specialist Killed in Vietnam Asks President John F. Kennedy 'If a War is Worth Fighting—Isn't It Worth Fighting to <u>Win</u>?' & President Kennedy Responds. February 18, 1963 and March 6, 1963." Reprinted with permission of Andrew Carroll. In it, Bobbie Lou Pendergrass writes to President Kennedy about her brother, one of the first casualties in Vietnam, with a longing to square her brother's death with the cause of war. She uses a direct but respectful tone and plain, assertive diction (391–392):

Dear President Kennedy,          February 18, 1963

My brother, Specialist James Delmas McAndrew, was one of the seven crew members killed on January 11 in a Viet Nam helicopter crash. . . . Jim went into the Marines as soon as he was old enough and was overseas for a long time. During those war years and even all during the Korean conflict we worried . . . but that was all very different. They were wars that our country were fighting, and everyone here knew that our sons and brothers were giving their lives for our country.

I can't help but feel that giving one's life for one's country is one thing, but being sent to a country where half our country never even heard of and being shot at without even a chance to shoot back is another thing altogether!

Can the small number of our boys over in Viet Nam possibly be doing enough good to justify the awful number of casualties? . . . If a war is worth fighting—isn't it worth fighting to win?

Please answer this and help me and my family to reconcile ourselves to our loss and to feel that even though Jim died in Viet Nam—and it isn't our war—it wasn't in vain. I am a good Democrat—and I'm not criticizing. I think you are doing a wonderful job—and God Bless You—
Very sincerely,
Bobbie Lou Pendergrass

Upon examining her letter, specifically the diction and the tone, we notice her facts giving way in the end to her real feelings of pride. Her voice is still determined by the rhetorical situation, which in her case is that she is writing to the president about a topic that is extraordinarily sensitive; hence, she uses an honest, expressive voice which progressively becomes less distant from the president and rises to fulfill her longing—to make sense of her brother's death in a chaotic war by turning to the only person who can respond to her pain—President Kennedy. Her audience is, thus, President Kennedy, and her context is the home front experiencing the effects of the Vietnam War.

The following letter is President Kennedy's response (392–393). In it he moves from the formal tone of a standard condolence letter to a more personal one—he uses the pronoun "I" often as he speaks from his heart:

Dear Mrs. Pendergrass:          March 6, 1963

I would like to express to you my deep and sincere sympathy in the loss of your brother. I can, of course, well understand your bereavement and the feelings which prompted you to write.

Americans are in Viet Nam because we have determined that this country must not fall under Communist domination. [*He continues with history of decision.*]

Your brother was in Viet Nam because the threat to the Vietnamese people is, in the long run, a threat to the Free World community, and ultimately a threat to us also.

I have written to you at length because I know that it is important to you to understand why we are in Viet Nam. James McAndrew must have foreseen that his service could take him into a war like this; a war in which he took part not as a combatant but as an advisor.

I believe if you can see this as he must have seen it, you will believe as he must have believed, that he did not die in vain.

Again, I would like to express to you and the members of your family my deepest personal sympathy. Sincerely, John F. Kennedy

Given the tenuous rhetorical situation, President Kennedy used a formal and moderately expressive voice; his voice was determined by the tragedy. This, in contrast to his first draft, which was more officious:

> Why did [your brother] have to prove his belief in a war which is not our own? That I can answer with certainty. We must continue to express our belief that every man has the God-given right to freedom, and we must continue to help those whom we can. We must not, however, spend our strength recklessly in danger of provoking a world conflict which could destroy our friends, our enemies, and ourselves. (394)

The following are pieces of writing in which writers' voices are reflected in diction, tone, and point of view.

### Example 3 Diction

"As Carbon Dioxide Grows, Tropical Trees Do Not" by Elizabeth Harball and Climatewire in *Scientific American*.

Scientists had assumed that trees would use increasing concentrations of $CO_2$ to grow more but research shows that is not the case.

Trees are definitely our allies when it comes to taking in greenhouse gases and thus aiding in the fight against climate change. But new research suggests that forests might not be quite as helpful as we'd hoped.

Computer models that predict how climate change will play out assume that as greenhouse gas concentrations go up, forests will take advantage of the additional carbon dioxide and grow a bit more, increasing their capacity to mitigate global warming.

But after analyzing tens of thousands of tree rings taken from tropical forests in Bolivia, Cameroon, and Thailand, an international team of scientists is calling this assumption into question.

Their research, published yesterday in the journal *Nature Geoscience*, found no correlation between increased atmospheric carbon dioxide concentrations over the past 150 years and forest growth as evidenced in trees' rings (Harball & Climateware):

Harball speaks from a primarily third-person point of view (with exception of "our allies" and "we'd hoped"), thus revealing a voice that is formal with a touch of the personal. The diction of the factual, research article with a scientific topic discloses not only a voice that speaks facts but also one that has an affectionate feeling toward the trees and a fear of climate change.

### Example 4
*Point of View*

Friedman, Thomas L. *The World Is Flat: A Brief History of the Twenty-First Century*. New York: Farrar, Straus, and Giroux, 2005.

> I had come to Bangalore, India's Silicon Valley, on my own Columbus-like journey of exploration. Columbus sailed with the *Nina*, the *Pinta*, and the *Santa Maria* in an effort to discover a shorter, more direct route to India by heading west, across the Atlantic, on what he presumed to be an open sea route to the East Indies—rather than going south and east around Africa, as Portuguese explorers of his day were trying to do. India and the magical Spice Islands of the East were famed at the time for their gold, pearls, gems, and silk—a source of untold riches. Finding this shortcut by the sea to India, at a time when the Muslim powers of the day had blocked the overland routes from Europe, was a way for both Columbus and the Spanish monarchy to become wealthy and powerful. When Columbus set sail, he apparently assumed the Earth was round, which was why he was convinced that he could get to India by going west. He miscalculated the distance, though. He thought the Earth was a smaller sphere than it is. He also did not anticipate running into a landmass before he reached the East Indies. Nevertheless, he called the aboriginal peoples he encountered in the new world "Indians." Returning home, though, Columbus was able to tell his patrons,

King Ferdinand and Queen Isabella, that although he never did find India, he could confirm that the world was indeed round. (Friedman 4)

Is Friedman's voice informal, formal, or in-between? Prove your point with evidence from the excerpt. Which rhetorical element—diction, tone, or point of view—does Friedman emphasize?

### Example 5
*Tone*
Rice, Condoleezza. *No Greater Honor: A Memoir of My Years in Washington*. New York: Random House, 2011.

Three days later, the President and I stood in the Oval for a few minutes alone before heading into the Roosevelt Room for the announcement. What an unlikely pair: a scion of a Republican political dynasty—albeit one with a Texas accent—and a middleclass black daughter of the South. We'd been through a lot since that meeting in Kennebunkport. Cataclysmic events and our response to them had shaped his presidency thus far. Now, with the dust settling, we had a chance to build a firm foundation for U.S. foreign policy in the changed circumstances of the post-9/11 world. I listened closely to the President's remarks as he introduced me to the press as his nominee for secretary of state. But frankly, I didn't want to listen too closely and become observably emotional. After he finished, I said a few words—very few—and returned to the Oval with him. "Go get 'em," he said. I laughed and said, "Yes, sir!" and left for Capitol Hill to begin the process known colloquially as confirmation. (Rice 295)

Rice speaks from a first-person point of view, revealing a voice that is personal, yet formal.

### Exercise 1
What do you observe about the diction and tone in the following excerpt from Marja Mills' book about Harper Lee, author of *To Kill a Mockingbird*, and her sister Alice?

Mills recounts an experience from her time with Harper "Nelle" Lee and sister Alice in Monroeville, Alabama:

We passed the occasional gas station and general store with "Coca-Cola" in fading white script on peeling red paint. We stopped at one of them. It was the kind of place that looked like it might still have Coke in those little six-and-a-half-ounce Coca-Cola bottling operation in Black River Falls, Wisconsin. I checked. No, even here it was cans and plastic bottles only. Next to the cash register and the March of Dimes box was a giant plastic jar of hard-boiled eggs in vinegar. Beside that was another big jar with something vaguely pink floating in the brine. Pickled-pigs feet. I'd never tasted either. I'd stick to Diet Coke for now.

(Mills 9)

- Mills, Marja. *The Mockingbird Next Door: Life with Harper Lee*. New York: Penguin Press, 2014.
- Is Mills' voice informal, formal, or in-between? Prove your point with evidence from the excerpt.
- Which rhetorical element—diction, tone, or point of view—does Mills emphasize?

### Exercise 2
In another letter recorded in *War Letters*, "Black Hawk Pilot Michael Durant writes from captivity in Somalia to assure his wife and one-year-old son that, although injured, he is still alive." Carroll provides the following background information on Durant.

On October 3, 1993, a Black Hawk helicopter flown by thirty-two-year-old CWO (Chief Warrant Officer) Michael Durant was shot out of the sky by a rocket-propelled grenade. The attack on Durant and his crew came during a U.S. attempt in Somalia to apprehend the "lieutenant" of clan leader Mohamed Farah Aidid. Knocked temporarily unconscious by the crash, Durant realized . . . [he had] a broken back and a leg that had snapped apart on impact. Immobilized by his injuries, Durant was unable to escape. [The Somalis] killed the last of his crew. . . . [And] beating him savagely, several Somalis decided the American pilot might be worth more alive than dead. . . . Guarded by Aidid's propaganda minster . . . Durant was allowed to write a single, brief letter to his wife and one-year-old son in Clarksville, Tennessee. (Carroll)

The following is Durant's letter:

Dear Lorrie & Joey:
I know you must be worried how I am doing. They are treating me well. The Somali doctor comes every day and cleans my injuries. The people taking care of me also are treating me well. They get whatever kind of food I ask for but there is no pizza available unfortunately. I want nothing more in the world than to be with you and Joey again. I see his face and I

pray that this will turn out OK. Please tell everyone else in the family that I hear their prayers and thing will work out OK.

Nothing else matters more to me than to see my family again. I think I will, I really do. You stay positive and be strong and give Joey more hugs and kisses for his Dad that misses him so.

I broke my leg (compound fracture right femur) and injured my back in the crash. I think my nose is broken but it does not hurt. I have a superficial gunshot wound in my left arm. The leg & back are the only real problems but as I said the medical care has been very good.

I hope to see you soon and I pray for the others who are missing, Ray, Bill, Tommy, and anyone else. I love you.

As a postscript, Carroll provides more details: "After the United States negotiated a peace with Aidid's militia, Durant, having spent ten days in captivity, was released. American forces withdrew from Somalia six months later" (467–469).

Which rhetorical element—diction, tone, or point of view—does Durant emphasize? How would you characterize his voice?

What are the elements of the rhetorical situation in the excerpt from *War Letters* given above?

• writer
• primary audience
• secondary audience
• topic/message
• purpose
• context
• text

# Chapter 6

# Stylistics

## ESSENTIALS

*What is "style" in writing?* Style refers to writers' choices that reveal unique ways of expression; being unique, a writer's style, like fingerprints, is recognizable. By writing with an arresting style, writers keep the interest of their audiences. Style includes figurative and literal language. *What is the difference?*

Figurative language: connotative words or phrases to emphasize, clarify, compare, or contrast points.

Figures of speech

- are common in figurative language, which is decorative and expresses ideas flavorfully. Metaphorically, figurative
- language is chocolate fudge, whereas literal language is vanilla ice cream. Literal language: denotative, original meanings
- found beside words in dictionaries.

Figurative language is more indirect than literal language. The former includes figures of speech, especially metaphors and similes. These figures of speech are not confined to poetry as they are also effective in nonfiction writing.

To study a writer's style, first examine "form and meaning"—also referred to as "method and message" or "craft and understanding." For instance, in his short story, "Soldier's Home," Ernest Hemingway wrote the following about his character Krebs who left Oklahoma to serve in a war:

He did not want any consequences. He did not want any consequences ever again. He wanted to live long without consequences.

Besides, he did not really need a girl. The army had taught him that. It was all right to pose as though you had to have a girl. Nearly everybody did that. But it wasn't true. You did not need a girl. That was the funny thing. (283)

Hemingway's writing shows an intersection between form (short, expressive sentences with words common to all of them), subject (verb and direct object), and meaning (a soldier who asserts his need not to get hurt romantically, while reassuring himself that advice from the army about relationships with women is untrue). The brief bursts of defensive thought—the form—matches the meaning—a vulnerable soldier.

*How is style achieved to ensure an effect or outcome?*

Writing *form* includes these features at the sentence level:

- Arrangement of words, sentences, and paragraphs

Diction (types of word choices)

Formal/Informal
General/Specific
Monosyllabic/Polysyllabic Syllables
Technical/Nontechnical

## Figures of Speech

Length of sentences
Point of view
Position of emphasis in sentence (beginning, middle, or end)
Punctuation

Syntax (organization of words in sentences—patterns and rules, following or deviating from them)
• Transitions
Types of sentences (simple, compound, compound-complex, complex; periodic, loose)

## FIGURES OF SPEECH

### Essentials

*What is a figure of speech?* A figure of speech is a play on words or, in other words, wordplay.

Since they could not rely on the written word, the Greeks invented figures of speech so that philosophers such as Aristotle, Plato, and Socrates could ensure their audiences would listen to and remember their orations or speeches. In modern times too, figuring or *configuring* speech refers to clever ways of using phrases so that audiences may understand and remember. As a writer, you should be asking, "Why are these words worth noticing?"

Figures of speech in writing help to create particular effects. Examples of these include the following:

## EFFECTS ON AUDIENCES

• Assenting to argument
• Changing perspective
• Creating of charm and interest
• Reflecting, negotiating position, and taking action
• Remembering messages more often
• Responding to Pathos (positive or negative): joy, hope, satisfaction, or dismay, sadness, dissatisfaction

## FIGURES OF SPEECH

### Schemes: Word Variation

Changes in Word Order:

*Anastrophe:* Rearrangement of the typical sentence pattern: subject-verb-object to, for example, object-subject-verb.
For example, "I walked up the door, / Shut the stairs, /Said my shoes, / Took off my prayers, / Turned off my bed, / Got into the light, / All Because, / You kissed me goodnight" (Natalie Dorsch).

"Ready are you? What know you of ready? For eight hundred years have I trained Jedi. My own counsel will I keep on who is to be trained. . . . This one a long time have I watched. . . . Never his mind on where he was" (Yoda, *Star Wars Episode V: The Empire Strikes Back*).
*Archaism:* Use of an older or obsolete form.
For example, "It is an ancient Mariner, / And he stoppeth one of three. / By thy long grey beard and glittering eye, / Now wherefore stopp'st thou me?" (Samuel Taylor Coleridge).
*Asyndeton:* Omission of conjunctions between a series of clauses.
For example, "Are all thy conquests, glories, triumphs, spoils, / Shrunk to this little measure?" (William Shakespeare, *Julius Caesar*).
*Ellipsis:* Omission of a word or words readily implied by context.
For example, "Wise men talk because they have something to say; fools, because they have to say something" (Plato).
*Hyperbaton:* the use of a word order other than the expected or usual order to emphasize latter part of phrases or sentences.
For example, "The right is ours. Have it, we must. Use it, we will" (Elizabeth Cady Stanton).
*Polysyndeton:* Using extra conjunctions in a series. Opposite of asyndeton.
For example, "There were frowzy fields, and cowhouses, and dunghills, and dustheaps, and ditches, and gardens, and summer-houses, and carpet-beating grounds, at the very door of the Railway. Little tumuli of oyster shells in the oyster season, and of lobster shells in the lobster season, and of broken crockery and faded cabbage leaves in all seasons, encroached upon its high places" (Charles Dickens).
*Tautology:* Repetition of an idea in different words, phrases, or sentences.
For example, "With malice toward none, with charity for all" (Abraham Lincoln).

Opposition:

*Antithesis:* Opposite ideas expressed in parallel form.
For example, "You don't make peace with friends. You make it with very unsavory enemies" (Yitzhak Rabin).

# TROPES: IDEA VARIATION

Inversions of Meaning
  *Emphasis*:

*Rhetorical Question:* Asking a question for a purpose other than obtaining the information requested.
For example, "How can the poor feel they have a stake in a system which says that the rich have due process but the poor may not?" (Ethel Kennedy).

*Irony:* Using language in such a way as to convey a meaning opposite of what the terms used denote (often by exaggeration). Three types:
- *Verbal:* A statement in which what is said is different from what is meant. For example, "Clear as mud."
- *Situational:* A situation in which the outcome is different from what is expected. For example, "A pilot with a fear of heights."
- *Dramatic:* Audience is aware of forthcoming events before the characters.

For example, in William Shakespeare's *Macbeth*, Macbeth plans the murder of Duncan while feigning loyalty. Duncan does not know of Macbeth's plans but the audience does.

*Oxymoron:* Placing two ordinarily opposing terms adjacent to one another. A compressed paradox.
For example, "darkness visible" (John Milton).

*Paradox:* An apparently contradictory statement that contains a measure of truth.
For example, "All animals are equal, but some are more equal than others" (George Orwell).

One Thing Associated with Another

*Allusion:* Reference to knowledge from literature, religion, philosophy, politics, mythology, history, or geography that audience is expected to know without immediate explanations.
  For example, "The rise in poverty will unlock a Pandora's box of crimes."

*Metaphor:* Reference to one thing as another, implying a comparison. An implied comparison between things that are essentially unlike. One thing is spoken of as if it were another. A mental construction of "blended space": base (foundation) and crown. Three types:

*Personal (Personified):*
  For example, "Melancholy is a resting place for all other emotions. / My love is a lavender rose in the winter" (John Donne).

*Symbolic (Abstract):*
  For example, "She wears her clothes as if they were thrown on with a pitchfork" (Jonathan Swift).

*Fantastical (Invented or Imagined):*
  For example, "The fog comes / on little cat feet. / It sits looking / over harbor and city / on silent haunches / and then moves on" (Carl Sandburg).

*Simile:* Explicit comparison of one thing to another using "like" or "as."

For example, "I would have given anything for the power to soothe her frail soul, tormenting itself in its invincible ignorance like a small bird beating about the cruel wires of a cage" (Joseph Conrad).

Examples of speech with schemes and tropes: "Woman's Rights to the Suffrage" by Susan B. Anthony (1820–1906). This speech was delivered in 1873, after Anthony was arrested, tried, and fined $100 for voting in the 1872 presidential election.

Friends and Fellow Citizens: I stand before you tonight under indictment for the alleged crime of having voted at the last presidential election, without having a lawful right to vote. It shall be my work this evening to prove to you that in thus voting, I not only committed no crime, but, instead, simply exercised my citizen's rights, guaranteed to me and all United States citizens by the National Constitution, beyond the power of any State to deny.

The *preamble* of the *Federal Constitution* says:

"We, the people of the United States, in order to form a more perfect union, establish justice, insure domestic tranquility, provide for the common defense, promote the general welfare, and secure the blessings of liberty to ourselves and our posterity, do ordain and establish this Constitution for the United States of America."

It was we, the people; not we, the white male citizens; nor yet we, the male citizens; but we, the whole people, who formed the Union. And we formed it, not to give the blessings of liberty, but to secure them; not to the half of ourselves and the half of our posterity, but to the whole people—women as well as men. And it is a downright mockery to talk to women of their enjoyment of the blessings of liberty while they are denied the use of the only means of securing them provided by this democratic-republican government—the ballot.

For any State to make sex a qualification that must ever result in the disfranchisement of one entire half of the people is to pass a bill of attainder, or an ex post facto law, and is therefore a violation of the supreme law of the land. By it the blessings of liberty are forever withheld from women and their female posterity. To them this government has no just powers derived from the consent of the governed. To them this government is not a democracy. It is not a republic. It is an odious aristocracy; a hateful oligarchy of sex; the most hateful aristocracy ever established on the face of the globe; an oligarchy of wealth, where the right govern the poor. An oligarchy of learning, where the educated govern the ignorant, or even an oligarchy of race, where the Saxon rules the African, might be endured; but this oligarchy of sex, which makes father, brothers, husband, sons, the oligarchs over the mother and sisters, the wife and daughters of every household—which ordains all men sovereigns, all women subjects, carries dissension, discord and rebellion into every home of the nation.

Webster, Worcester and Bouvier all define a citizen to be a person in the United States, entitled to vote and hold office.

The only question left to be settled now is—Are women persons? And I hardly believe any of our opponents will have the hardihood to say they are not. Being persons, then, women are citizens; and no State has a right to make any law, or to enforce any old law, that shall abridge their privileges or immunities. Hence, every discrimination against women in the constitutions and laws of the several States is today null and void, precisely as in every one against Negroes.

Susan B. Anthony's Speech: "After Being Convicted of Voting in the 1872 Presidential Election," americanrhetoric.org, Monroe County, New York, 1873

***Exercise 1***

Identify the figures of speech present in the following examples (some of the examples contain figures of speech that have been listed in the Instructors Guide):

"Laugh and the world laughs with you" (Ella Wheeler Wilcox) _____
_____

"We shall fight on the beaches, we shall fight on the landing grounds, we shall fight on the fields and in the streets, we shall fight in the hills" (Winston Churchill). _____
_____
_____
_____
_____

"Progress is not proclamation nor palaver. It is not pretense nor play on prejudice. It is not the perturbation of the people passion-wrought, nor a promise proposed" (Warren G. Harding) _____
_____

**Table 6.1   Rhetorical Situation of "The Preamble"**

| Primary Audience | Purpose | Rhetorical Appeal | Techniques to Persuade the Audience | Effects of Techniques to Persuade Audience |
|---|---|---|---|---|
| Governing Body of U.S. (Male Representatives) | To persuade governing body to allow women to vote. | Logos | Allusion "The preamble of the Federal Constitution" Syncrisis (SIN-crih-sis) "The not-that-but-this figure" Repetition of "we" Rhetorical Question | Cites official document, specifically rules that support her gender argument. Contrast in logical manner; women are "fellow citizens" but not allowed same freedom; highlighting double standards to weaken them as plausible; dismisses information directly following "not"; emphasizes information directly following Argues principles of fairness and seeks to persuade primary audience that woman are one-half of "we" Poignant question of which there is only one ethical answer. |
| Women of voting age, in particular; all females, in general. | To inspire | Pathos | Isocolon | Amplifies emotional response: anger at devaluation of women as fellow citizens. Rallies against "oligarchy." |

_____ "Rome has spoken; the case is concluded" (St. Augustine). _____

"Her voice is full of money" (F. Scott Fitzgerald).

_____ "A cathedral, a wave of a storm, a dancer's leap, never turn out to be as high as we had hoped" (Marcel Proust). _____

"Unless hours were cups of sack, and minutes capons, and clocks the tongues of bawds, and dials the signs of leaping houses, and the blessed sun himself a fair hot wench in flame-color'd taffeta, I see no reason why thou shouldst be so superfluous to demand the time of day" (Shakespeare, Hamlet, IV. 1.2.7). _____

_____ "But passion lends them power, time means, to meet" (Shakespeare, *Romeo and Juliet*, II. Prol. 13). _____

"From such crooked wood as that which man is made of, nothing straight can be fashioned" (Immanuel Kant). _____

"Was this the face that launched a thousand ships, / And burnt the topless towers of Ilium?" (Christopher Marlowe). _____

"Love is an irresistible desire to be irresistibly desired" (Robert Frost). _____

"She was not quite what you would call refined. She was not quite what you would call unrefined. She was the kind of person that keeps a parrot" (Mark Twain).

"Why I should fear I know not, / Since guiltiness I know not; but yet I feel I fear" (Shakespeare, *Othello*, 5.2.38). _____

"If thou hast any sound, or use of voice, / Speak to me. / If there be any good thing to be done, / That may to thee do ease and grace to me, / Speak to me" (Shakespeare, *Hamlet*, 1.1.128). _____

"A man may devote himself to death and destruction to save a nation; but no nation will devote itself to death and destruction to save mankind" (Samuel Taylor Coleridge). _____

"He [von Stauffenberg, a leader for the plot] was the man who unmistakably wore the mantle of a near-mystic German past, a warrior Germany, a noble Germany, a poetic Germany, a Germany of myth and longing" (Justin Cartwright). _____

### Exercise 2
Composing Your Own Schemes and Tropes:

*What is the benefit of using schemes and tropes in your writing?* While no English instructor advocates using a voice full of hyperbatons—similar to Yoda's—in your academic papers, and some of the figures of speech are more common in poetry than in prose, a fair use of antimetabole, epistrophe, and polysyndeton will give your written word a richer style.

For the following topics, create three figures of speech in the schemes category and three figures of speech in the tropes category.

• character on television series or film
• delicious meal
• ocean: snorkeling, or scuba diving

### Exercise 3
Locate figures of speech in excerpts from the following famous speech of Cal Ripkin, Jr. Next, explain the effects of Ripkin's figures of speech on his audience: fans of all ages.

Cal Ripken, Jr., "Farewell to Baseball Address," October 6, 2001, Camden Yards, Baltimore, Maryland

As a kid, I had this dream.

And I had the parents that helped me shape that dream.

Then, I became part of an organization, the Baltimore Orioles—the Baltimore Orioles, to help me grow that dream. Imagine playing for my hometown team for my whole career.

And I have a wife and children to help me share and savor the fruits of that dream.

And I've had teammates who filled my career with unbelievable moments.

**Table 6.2  Exercise 3 Application**

| Figures of Speech | Effects on Audience |
| --- | --- |
| Anaphora | Receptive to Ripkin's expressing of gratitude |

And you fans, who have loved the game, and have shared your love with me.

Tonight, we close a chapter of this dream—my playing career. But I have other dreams.

You know, I might have some white hair on top of this head—well, maybe on the sides of this head. But I'm really not that old.

My dreams for the future include pursuing my passion for baseball. Hopefully, I will be able to share what I have learned. And, I would be happy if that sharing would lead to something as simple as a smile on the face of others.

One question I've been repeatedly asked these past few weeks is, "How do I want to be remembered?" My answer has been simple: to be remembered at all is pretty special.

I might also add that if, if I am remembered, I hope it's because, by living my dream, I was able to make a difference. Thank you. ("Farewell")

## SENTENCE VARIATION

### Essentials

*What is important to know about sentences?* Often, student writers pay more attention to content rather than sentences in their academic essays. Unless they are writing fiction, that is, poetry and short stories, and are particularly creative with words, they focus more on ideas than syntax (sentence structure). Readers also focus on content because they like ideas and information and pay less attention to sentences except when they are either well-crafted or bumpy. Writing sentences that are smooth creates an engaging and fluid reading experience.

*How do you know when a sentence is a sentence (not a fragment)?* To ensure that a group of successive words is a sentence, the words will fill the blank in a test frame such as "They refused to believe the idea that_____" or "It is known that_____" Example 1: They refused

to believe the idea that the Earth is flat (sentence). Example 2: It is known that visited Barcelona and saw Christopher Columbus statue. (fragment)

*Why vary your sentence patterns?* To "shake up" dull and repetitive writing. To avoid boring the reader. To avoid sounding like an amateur. Sentence length can have a great effect on your readers as well as your message to them. Accomplished by writing clear prose with powerful verbs, the goal of varying the sentence patterns is to keep your reader engaged with your argument.

*What are examples of unskillful writing?*

- Sentences repeatedly beginning with demonstrative pronouns: that, there, this, those
- Repeating sentence patterns: for instance, the pattern of subject, verb, direct object
- Sentences repeatedly beginning with articles: a, an, the.

*How can you vary your sentences?* Think of attaining this skill as a personal challenge, one which will require you to press, as you seek to improve your sentences, the "pause" button repeatedly in the final phases of your writing process. Today's readers are bombarded with information. As a result, they want to read clear, direct writing that has powerful verbs and well-edited sentences. If readers have to work too hard, they tend to "turn off" and stop reading.

*When are simple sentences appropriate?* There is a place for complex sentences, and there is a place for simple sentences. Clear writing often involves a combination of both. The decision whether to use simple or complex sentences depends on the rhetorical situation: audience, purpose, and context. For example, writing a manual with directions to activate a cell phone for an audience of adults with limited technical knowledge will require simple sentences while writing an argument to improve snow removal in a letter to the town council will require more complex sentences.

*Which famous authors wrote deceptively simple sentences?* Some of the greatest literary writers, including Amy Tan (*Joy Luck Club*), Harper Lee (*To Kill a Mockingbird*), and Ernest Hemingway (*The Old Man and the Sea*), wrote in simple language with clear, direct sentences although the content was sophisticated. An example from *The Old Man and the Sea* shows this:

> The old man was thin and gaunt with deep wrinkles in the back of his neck. The brown blotches of the benevolent skin cancer the sun brings from its reflection on the tropic sea were on his cheeks. The blotches ran well down the sides of his face and his hands had the deep-creased scars from handling heavy fish on the cords. But none of these scars were fresh. They were as old as erosions in a fishless desert. (2)

Simple sentences such as these may convey complex meaning. In this excerpt, the old man's physical appearance hides his strength.

*What are different ways to vary your sentences?* (1) Type, (2) Syntax, (3) Patterns, and (4) Length

1. *Types*
A. Declarative (assertions), exclamatory (expressions!), imperative (commands), and interrogative (questions)

Example 1

- Declarative: The United States has sent men and women military members into combat overseas to protect our freedom at home.
- Exclamatory: Soldiers fired bullets for twenty-eight continuous minutes!
- Imperative: We must examine the casualty rates from the past two wars.
- Interrogative: Why do we need to send more troops to war?

2. *Syntax*:
A. Forms and Loose/Periodic Sentences
*What is the difference between a phrase and a clause?*

Phrase: Collection of words that contain noun(s) *and* verb(s); the noun does not function as a subject. For example: leaving our old house behind

Clause: Collection of words that contains a noun (functioning as a subject) *or* a verb For example: Our

old house is still surrounded by the same decrepit fence.

Example 2

> ***Forms*: Simple, Compound, Complex, and Compound-Complex Terms:**
> IC = Independent Clause
> DC = Dependent Clause
> CC = Coordinating Conjunction (FANBOYS: for, and, nor, but, or, yet, so)

- Simple (IC): Citizens wave flags.
- Compound (IC +, CC + IC): Citizens wave flags, and their flags fly proudly.
- Complex (IC +, DC or DC, + IC) Citizens wave flags, since they are proud. Or: Since they are proud, citizens wave flags.
- Compound-Complex (ICs + , DC or DC, + ICs):

Citizens wave flags, for they want to display their views and emotions prominently, since they are driven by reasons relating to national pride.
(IC, + IC + , DC)
Since they are driven by reasons related to national pride, citizens wave flags for they want to display their views and emotions prominently.
(DC + IC + IC)
*Loose (L) or Periodic (PE)*

Example 3
Loose: Edith Mayo, a curator of political history at the Smithsonian Institution, was responsible for the reinterpretation of the First Ladies exhibit at a time when funding was scarce and research grants were impossible to find.

Periodic: "To believe your own thought, to believe that what is true for you in your private heart is true for all men, that is genius" (Ralph Waldo Emerson).

### Exercise 4
Which type of sentence (loose or periodic)v is exhibited below?_____

"And the letter had broken my father's heart so much—these daughters calling my mother from another life he never knew—that he gave the letter to my mother's old friend Auntie Lindo and asked her to write back and tell my sisters, in the greatest way possible, that my mother was dead" (Amy Tan).

*Patterns*: Branching, Parts of Speech, Openings, and Closings
*Branching*: Left, Mid-, Right

Left: *Developed in the early twentieth century*, the bicycle transported people to social activities.
Mid-: The bicycle, *developed in the early twentieth century*, transported people to social activities.
Right: The bicycle transported people to social activities *after its development in the early twentieth century*.

---

**Parts of Speech:**
S = Subject; V = Verb; LV = Linking Verb; Adj: Adjective; O = Object (Direct or Prepositional); IO = Indirect Object; OC = Object Complement (noun, pronoun, or adjective following a direct object and renames the direct object)

---

Potential Patterns: S-V, S-V-O, S-LV-N, S-LV-Adj, S-AV-IO-DO, S-V-O-OC, S-V-O- Adj., S-V-O-Adv.

Example 4

S-V: The nurses worked.
S-V-O: The nurses helped *patients*. (direct object).
S-V-O: The nurses helped patients in the *hospital*. (object of preposition)
S-LV-N: The nurses were educators.
LV-Adj: The nurses were helpful.
S-AV-IO-DO: The nurses rapidly brought patients food.
S-V-O-OC: The nurses treated Juan, the soldier.
S-V-O-Adj: The nurses found the wounds abundant.
S-V-O-Adv: The nurses wrapped bandages tightly.

*Openings of Sentences*: Phrases or Clauses: adverbial, adjectival, appositive, infinitive, preposition, or participial.

Example 5

*Adverbial Clause*: When volunteering for their country, students are involved at the community, state, and national levels.
*Adjectival Clause*: Whoever volunteered for extra clean-up duty will earn recognition at a local ceremony.

*Appositive*: The volunteers, an energetic group of students, cleared debris from the beach in only two hours.
*Infinitive*: To volunteer is a selfless act by students.
*Preposition*: After one week, the volunteers had finished the work on the beach, despite hail and windy conditions. *Participial*: Cleaning up the beach, the volunteers encountered crabs, jellyfish, and starfish.

Example 6
*Closing Sentences:* Incrementum (series of equal items that lead to summary statement at end) or Periodic.

Incrementum: Once revised and adopted in 1960, the American flag had thirteen red, horizontal stripes representing the first states of the Union; blue rectangle in the canton, or upper left corner; fifty small white, five-point stars representing the fifty states in nine horizontal rows alternating between six and five stars per row.

Periodic: A gesture, a symbol, a slogan, this great representation of patriotism involves every state in the nation, every historical event since 1777: the American flag.

Example 7
The following is an excerpt from freshman Ava's rhetorical analysis of Lyndon B. Johnson's speech, "We Shall Overcome," followed by an analysis of Ava's writing style that brings together different approaches to sentences.

On March 5th, 1965, Lyndon Baines Johnson delivered a speech in Congress entitled "We Shall Overcome," an appeal for civil rights for people of all races and the upholding of "the dignity of man and the destiny of democracy" (Johnson 1). He addressed his primary audience as "Mr. Speaker, Mr. President, Members of Congress" (1), but also acknowledged his secondary audience as all Americans in general—"every member of both parties, Americans of all religions and of all colors, from every section of this country" (1). Johnson aptly utilized kairos in delivering his speech on this day, eight days after the bloody Selma to Montgomery marches took place, during which civil rights supporters were violently massacred. The issue of civil rights was a controversial and captivating topic in America, and Americans had a highly vested interest in it, as it affected many aspects of daily life, from voting for a President, to attending segregated versus integrated schools, or taking a seat on a bus ride home.

- Number of sentences: four
- Number of words in sentences: range between thirty-nine to fifty words; average: forty per sentence.
- Sentence form: two compound-complex; two complex
- Sentence types: four declarations
- Voice: Active
- Openings: One prepositional phrase; three standard (S-V)
- Which conclusion to draw? Ava's writing exhibits complex thinking on paper.

### Exercise 5

Examine a paragraph from one of your recent papers. Reflect on these questions:

- What are your favored types of sentence syntax, patterns, and length?
- Why do you favor these types?

### Exercise 6

Label types of sentences (Simple, Compound, Complex, or Compound-Complex) in excerpt:

Work-Life Balance Is a Myth. Do This Instead" by
    Marcus Buckingham and Ashley Goodall
It seems more useful, then, to not try to balance the unbalanceable, but to treat work the same way you do life: By maximizing what you love. _____ Here's what we mean. _____ Consider why two people doing exactly the same work seem to gain strength and joy from very different moments. _____ When we interviewed several anesthesiologists, we found that while their title and job function are identical, the thrills and chills they feel in their job are not. _____ One said he loved the thrill of holding each patient hovering at that one precise point between life and death, while he shuddered at the "pressure" of helping each patient get healthy once the operation was complete. _____ Another said she loved the bedside conversations before the operation, and the calm sensitivity required to bring a sedated patient gently back to consciousness without the panic that afflicts many patients.

_____

Another was drawn mostly to the intricacies of the anesthetic mechanism itself and has dedicated herself to defining precisely how each drug does what it does. _____ Each one of us, for no good reason other than the clash of our chromosomes, draws strength from different activities, situations, moments and interactions.

_____

### Example 8

The following examples shows two sample sentences combined in six ways with various clauses and phrases.

Sample Sentences:

    The Vietnam Veterans Memorial Wall is dedicated to honoring those who died in the Vietnam War.

    The Wall is a place of healing for those affected by one of the most contentious wars in our nation's history.

- *Adjectival Clause*: **A place of healing**, the Vietnam Veterans Memorial Wall is dedicated to those who died in the Vietnam War.
- *Adverbial Clause*: **When visiting the Vietnam Veterans Memorial**, citizens realize a dedication to honor those who died in the Vietnam War.
- *Appositive Phrase*: The Vietnam Veterans Memorial Wall, **a dedication of honor**, recognizes those who died in the Vietnam War.
- *Infinitive Phrase*: **To dedicate** a memorial to those who died in the Vietnam war, the government erected the Vietnam Veterans Wall.
- *Prepositional Phrase*: **By honoring those who died in the Vietnam War**, the Vietnam Veterans Memorial Wall serves as a place of tribute and healing.
- *Participial Phrase*: **Affected by one of the most contentious wars in our nation's history**, soldiers, loved ones, and other citizens find the Wall a place of healing and honor.

### Exercise 7

Cinco de Mayo, or "the fifth of May," commemorates the victory of the Mexican army in 1862 over France at the Battle of Puebla. The holiday is minor in Mexico, but major in the United States where it serves as a celebration of Mexican culture and heritage including parades and Mariachi music festivals.

Sentences:

- *Adjectival Clause*:
- *Adverbial Clause*:
- *Appositive Phrase*:
- *Infinitive Phrase*:
- *Prepositional Phrase*:
- *Participial Phrase*:

### Exercise 8

Identify the types of openings: Phrases or Clauses—adverbial, adjectival, appositive, infinitive, preposition, or participial—in sentences from literary authors:

_____ *"Although they lived in style,* they felt always an anxiety in the house" (D. H. Lawrence).

_____ ". . . the watching, listening faces underwent a change, the eyes focusing on something within; the music seemed to soothe a poison out of the" (James Baldwin).

_____ Rachel Carson, *a biologist and writer*, published the novel *Silent Spring* in 1962.

_____ *"To err* is human; to forgive, divine" (*Alexander Pope*).

_____ *"On the pleasant shore off the French Riviera, about halfway between Marseilles and the Italian border* stands a large, proud, rose-colored hotel" (F. Scott Fitzgerald).

_____ *"Whirling happily in my starchy frock, showing off my biscuit-polished patent-leather shoes and lavender socks, tossing my head in a way that makes my ribbons bounce,* I stand, hands on hips, before my father" (Alice Walker).

*Chapter 7*

# Revision

## ESSENTIALS

*What is revision?* Revision is "re-envisioning" your draft to make your ideas clearer and responsive to the rhetorical situation surrounding your writing.

*What is a brief background on revision practices?* *Revisio* was not part of Aristotle's scheme because the Greek philosophers delivered speeches, which by their very nature could not be revised. Revision practices were added by later rhetoricians in the 1700s. More extensive revision practices, especially during the writing process, became common later in the 1900s. Today, revision is a common practice of writers.

*What are the two main areas to revise in papers?* Content and conventions. For purposes of this text, the focus is on revision at the sentence-level that impacts the greater meaning of a paper.

*Content* refers to the rhetorical situation:

* addressing instructor's *prompt*; answering your *guiding question*
* showing *audience* (primary) awareness
* fulfilling *purpose*
* conveying a clear *thesis statement*
* aligning *title*, *thesis statement*, and *topic sentences*
* writing a strong *introduction*
* providing adequate *context*
* providing convincing *evidence*
* integrating *quotes/paraphrases*
* writing a strong *conclusion*
* expressing *voice* in diction/tone appropriate for rhetorical situation*

*also considered under "Conventions" for vocabulary at the sentence-level

*Conventions* refer to sentence-level and format of writing, including the following:

* citations (in-text and Works Cited)
* *diction (also considered under "Content" for impact on meaning)
* format
* grammar
* punctuation
* spelling
* syntax
* transitions

*What is revising for economy of words?* This exercise is to reduce excess words. William Strunk, the well-regarded English professor of the 1920s, said:

> Vigorous writing is concise. A sentence should contain no unnecessary words, a paragraph no unnecessary sentences, for the same reason that a drawing should have no unnecessary lines and a machine no unnecessary parts. This requires not that the writer make all his sentences short, or that he avoid all detail and treat his subjects only in outline, but that every word tell. Strunk, William. *The Elements of Style: The Original Edition*. New York: SoHo Press, 2011. (Originally printed in 1923, Harcourt) (24)

*What are several tips for revising?*

* Take a break from your draft. Clear your head and begin again.
* Read your draft aloud, or ask a friend to read your draft to you.
* Imagine yourself as one of your readers, and the way they "experience" your writing.
* Ask a peer for feedback.

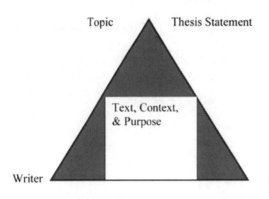

**Figure 7.1   Full Rhetorical Situation.**

*Exercise 1*

Below is a series of questions to ask yourself or a peer during revision process:

- Compare . . . and . . . with regard to . . .
- Do you agree or disagree with this statement . . .? Explain why . . . (Explain how . . . )
- How are . . . and . . .similar?
- How does . . . affect . . .?
- How is . . . related to . . . that we studied earlier?
- How would you use . . . to . . .?
- What are the strengths and weaknesses of . . .?
- What conclusions can you draw about . . .?
- What do you think causes . . .? Why?
- What do you think would happen if . . .?
- What evidence is there to support your answer?
- What is a new example of . . .?
- What is the difference between . . . and . . .?
- What is the main idea of . . .?
- What is the significance of . . .?
- Which . . . do you think is best and why?

*What are several techniques to improve sentence-level clarity?* There are many techniques. Below are several included in this text and in Instructors Guide online:

- Active/passive voice
- Given-New method of coherence
- Choosing exact words
- Transitional words

## ACTIVE AND PASSIVE VOICE

### Essentials

Read an excerpt of rather extreme passive voice from acclaimed French author Raymond Queneau used in his *Exercises in Style* (1981) to make the point about the "heaviness" of passive writing. In his text, Queneau wrote poetic versions of a conflict between two men on a bus in France, including this passive selection:

> It was midday. The bus was being got into by passengers. They were being squashed together. A hat was being worn on the head of a young gentlemen. . . . A long neck was one of the characteristics of the young gentlemen. The man standing next to him was being grumbled at by the latter because of the jostling which was being inflicted on him by him. As soon as a vacant seat was espied by the young gentlemen it was made the object of his precipitate movements and it became sat down upon. (72)

Queneau took poetic license and wrote passively in a wordplay exercise; the result shows his subjects: the bus, the seat, and the male rider as recipients, rather than agents, of the action. Similar to most writers, Queneau chose his words for effect, which resulted in labored writing that readers would find hard to sort through. Most writers would not write with such great extent, but Queneau's words remind us of the audience's frustrated experience when reading sentences with too much passive voice.

*How do writers define active and passive voice?* The "voice" of a verb shows whether the subject of the sentence performs the action or is acted upon. Active voice involves subjects (or agents, if referring to people) performing the action by using action verbs (e.g., *Protesters unified* their efforts to pass the regulation), whereas passive voice involves disguised, unknown, or relocated agents acted upon by "to be" and past participle verbs (e.g., Votes *are counted* by the volunteers). Helping verbs may also exist in passive expressions (e.g., Votes *have been counted* by the volunteers.). As shown in some passive expressions, the agent is an object in the prepositional phrase: by the volunteers. Passive expressions sometimes contain no agent (e.g., Votes *are counted*), indicating that the agent is unknown, unimportant, or unreported.

*What are the functions of verbs?* Verbs tell us what nouns do. Verbs express conditions or possessions. Verbs tell us what state a person or thing is in. Verbs are further classified into transitive and intransitive verbs.

*What does the "voice" of verbs mean?* Of all the parts of speech, only verbs have "voice," which refers to structure or form, not meaning. For instance, Louisa *placed* the quilt on the bed (active). The quilt *was placed upon the bed by Louisa* (passive). Though certain words have passive meanings, for example, sleep, injured, lied to, sit, and others, they are still categorized as action verbs if used in active-voice structures.

### Example 1

1. Passive Voice: Research *will be presented* by senior students at the conference.

    Active Voice: Senior students *will present* their research at the conference.
2. Passive Voice: The students' proposal to leave early for the holidays *is being considered* by the dean and her staff.

    Active Voice: Currently, the dean and her staff *consider* the students' proposal to leave early for the holidays.

*Why do writers and instructors generally favor active rather than passive voice?* Active voice is more direct and energized. Passive voice is often distracting to readers because the words feel heavy, and the pace feels slow. Some writers rely heavily on passive voice, which suggests low audience awareness.

*What are the different purposes of active and passive voice?* A closer look reveals more rhetorical purposes for active voice, and fewer for passive voice. To raise audience awareness, writers can ask themselves: Which arguments call for passive or active voice? Writers make choices about when to use which voice, which what Aristotle calls a "means of persuasion." The "means" refers to a writer's tools or strategies to persuade an audience: for example, diction (word choice), tone, sentence structure, and more. In Ancient Greece, Aristotle would have been referring to rhetorical appeals such as ethos, pathos, and logos—in other words, only the tools the philosophers could use orally.

*In which disciplines are active and passive voice acceptable?* In majors, such as the arts, business, education, and social sciences active voice is acceptable. In majors such as engineering, law, natural sciences, and technology, passive voice is a convention or requirement of legal documents and scientific documents, while active voice is common in narrative or other literary writing.

*What are transitive and intransitive verbs—and their relation to passive and active voice?*

### Example 2
Transitive Verbs/Passive Voice:

The letters were written by the soldiers.
My former classmates were seen at the reunion.
The lamp was broken on the way home.
Intransitive verbs/Active Voice (No Direct Object present)
Soldiers marched. (verb) Children giggled with pleasure. (adjective) She exited quickly. (adverb)

**Table 7.1  Active and Passive Voice**

| Features | Advantages | Disadvantages |
|---|---|---|
| **Passive Voice** | Fewer words | May offend readers with |
| Subject or agent ("doer") performs the action; subject is clear | Engages readers | directness |
| Action verbs | Direct | Names the agent ("doer") |
| Intransitive verb with no object. | Concise | when preference may be |
| (The Belle of Amherst *wrote*) | | concealment |
| **Active Voice** | Conceals | More words |
| Subject or agent is acted upon; subject is vague or absent | responsibility | Disengages readers |
| Auxiliary verb: "to be" and past participle of main verb (e.g., | Diminishes harshness | Indirect |
| "The species *are separated*.") | of message | Tedious |
| Transitive verb with object (The Belle of Amherst *wrote poems*). | Recipient of action is | Vague |
| A "by" phrase (present in some passive sentences) (e.g., "A lot of | emphasized | |
| money is always spent *by the students*. | | |

**Table 7.2  Intransitive and Transitive Verbs**

| Intransitive Verbs | Transitive Verbs |
|---|---|
| Action verbs: marched, hiked, researched, sang | Linking verbs: is, are, was, were, be, being, been |
| Does not requires a direct object (noun or pronoun) to complete its meaning | Requires a direct object (noun or pronoun) to complete its meaning. Direct object answers question: Who? or What? |
| Sentences end in verbs, adjectives, or adverbs | |
| Active Voice favors | Passive Voice favors |
| Show subject performing action | Show subject receiving action |

### Exercise 1

Circle verbs, and label as transitive or intransitive:

The director blocked the actors' movements for a particularly dramatic scene.

Due to her aching shoulder, Alison delegated her presentation to a coworker.

Recently, Taylor traveled to Alaska to photograph the wildlife and mountains.

Reciting their poems from memory, each poet performed superbly.

### Exercise 2

*Converting Passive to Active Voice*

1. Locate percentage of passive voice in a paper. See next page for checking "Readability Statistics" in *Word*.
2. Delete "to be" verbs: "be, been, and being" from your writing altogether; effective writing leaves these words in the dust. Use "Find" option in *Word* to locate these verbs. In "Search Document" box, put spaces before and after linking verbs so you do not see them within longer words. Ex. Become
3. Use fewer of these linking verbs: am, are, is, was, and were. Replace them with action verbs, which make your writing stronger and more "mobile." Use "Find" and "Replace" options in *Word* to locate linking verbs. In "Search Document" box, put spaces before and after linking verbs so you do not see them within longer words. Ex. Isis and Sam

   (*Note*: usage of "am, are, is, was, and were" does not always indicate passive voice if a subject complement is present.) For example:
4. Locate the subject, which is often the object of the prepositional phrase beginning with "by." Relocate object from preposition phrase" to place before action verb earlier in sentence.

   Care packages for troops were arranged *by freshmen students*.

   *Freshmen students* arranged care packages for troops.
5. If there is no prepositional phrase beginning with "by," identify and add the absent subject, that is, *who* or *what* is performing the action expressed in the verb.

   To save time, the research paper *was written* on a library computer.

   To save time, *Juan wrote* his research paper on a library computer.

   *Place subject in front of the verb/verb phrase to change the voice accordingly.

*What is "readability"?* The level of readers' understanding of writing; the minimum education level required for readers to comprehend the writing.

*How is readability assessed?* Readability checks for grade level, reading ease, and passive-voice percentage. Also, average number of syllables per word (word difficulty) and words per sentence (length).

Look for box with title: "Readability Statistics"; focus on section:

*How does a writer check "Readability Statistics" in Word?*

- Click: "File"
- Click: "Options"
- Click: "Proofing Tab"
- Look for "When correcting grammar and spelling"
- Check box of "Show readability statistics"
- Click: Settings
- Scroll down under "Grammar and Style" to "Style"
- Check box for "Passive Sentences"; this will
- Exit out of options; return to your document
- Complete a full "Spelling and Grammar" check

**Table 7.3  Non-Passive Sentences**

| Subject | Linking Verb | Subject Complement |
|---|---|---|
| The result | was | superb |
| Rents | are | high in NYC. |
| O'Hare | is | a chaotic airport. |

- Look for a "Readability Statistics" grey box on screen
  - Focus on lowest section with "Readability: Passive Sentences" (percentage)
  - "Flesch Reading Ease" (0–100)
  - "Flesch-Kincaid Grade Level" (K-17)

*How does a writer interpret passive voice percentage (from "Readability Statistics") in Word?*

The higher the percentage, the more passive voice phrases in document. The general rule of thumb:

> Strive for ≥ 10%, Passive Voice. As you make progress, strive for ≥ 5%. Always consider the level of your audience (Eleventh and twelfth graders? College students? Professionals? Senior citizens?) to whom you are directing your writing.

*Note*: If you want to check the passive-voice percentage of a portion of your document, highlight the selected text and press F7. When asked, "Do you want to check remainder of document?" select NO so that the displayed percentage relates only to selected portion.

### Exercise 3

Revise the following sentences with consideration of these questions: (1) How can the sentences become more effective? (Fewer words? Addition of action verbs? Relocation of the subject/agent?); (2) Which rhetorical purposes do they serve in contexts or rhetorical situations?

1. Listening to Marilyn Nelson recite her poetry had the effect of inspiring me to write a few stanzas.
2. In Tim O'Brien's novel *The Things They Carried,* the death of Ted Lavender, a soldier in his platoon, is something that Lt. Cross takes the blame for.
3. Westminster Abbey is the place where busts of famous literary figures are found.
4. Poets, novelists, and essayists were expected to attend the Booksellers' Convention.

*I have a dream* speech was delivered by Dr. Martin Luther King, Jr. during a turbulent time in the 1960s.

*What are rhetorical purposes for active and passive voice? In other words, why do writers purposefully use passive or active voice?*

a. *Quantity*; supports active voice

*Their Eyes Were Watching God* was written by Zora Neale Hurston. (passive voice sentence of eleven words)

Zora Neale Hurston wrote *Their Eyes Were Watching God*. (active voice sentence of nine words)

Rhetorical Purpose: Concise sentences with fewer words are more accessible and engaging to readers.

b. *Definition*; supports active voice

By definition, passive voice contains weaker "to be" verbs and active voice contains stronger action verbs.

- A Thanksgiving meal is being provided for the homeless by the students' efforts.
- Students coordinated an effort to provide a Thanksgiving meal for the homeless.

Rhetorical Purpose: Preceding action verbs, the agents are in a recognized position of performing the action.

c. *Position of emphasis*; supports either active or passive voice

In the making of a joke, the punch line is in the position of emphasis. The adage, "People tend to remember best what they hear last" certainly applies to jokes as well as the final words or phrases in sentences in writing.

- As I backed out of the driveway, a small brick wall encountered my car.
- As I backed out of the driveway, I hit a brick wall.

Rhetorical Purpose: By placing the brick wall in the position of emphasis, writers can either choose passive or active voice depending on the effect they are trying to achieve.

d. *Conceal or reveal the subject/agent*; supports either active or passive voice.

Concealment:

A politician argues, "Mistakes were made"

An usher warns, "If you do not cease talking in the movie theatre, you will be asked to leave."

Revelation:

A politician argues, "Our office personnel made mistakes in the accounting."

An usher warns, "If you do not cease talking in the movie theatre, I will ask you to leave."

Rhetorical Purpose: To suppress or promote the agent's responsibility.

e. *Subject/Agent is unimportant, unknown, or unreported*; supports passive voice.

In given contexts, passive voice is appropriate in writing or speaking:

1. Subject/Agent is unimportant    The poems were collected for the creative writing contest.
2. Subject/Agent is unknown    The university buildings were constructed in 1946.
3. Subject/Agent is better left unsaid    The textbooks were ordered for the wrong class.
   Rhetorical Purpose: To place the subject acted upon before the verb to emphasize its importance, rather than the agent.

### Example 3

Some of Shakespeare's greatest tragedies were written by him after the death of his young son Hamnet.

The writer's rhetorical purpose using passive voice is "Position of Emphasis" as she wants to "save the best for last" and place spotlight on Shakespeare's son, Hamnet, whose name has a different spelling than the namesake for his play *Hamlet*. Readers will take note of this unique fact, and the writer will succeed in bringing the audience's attention to "Hamnet," rather than Shakespeare himself whom everyone knows wrote tragedies. The rhetorical purpose will be fulfilled.

The objective is to use passive voice purposefully—if the rhetorical purpose and context are best served with this verb form.

### Exercise 4

For each of the following thesis statements: (1) decide the rhetorical purpose from list on previous page; (2) if relevant to the rhetorical purpose, convert passive to active voice.

1. Acid rain is caused by toxic chemicals, which are released into the air from the smokestacks of large manufacturing plants and, once they move into the clouds, these chemicals return to the earth in the form of rain.
   Rhetorical Purpose:_____
   _____
2. Every year, more and more oil is removed from the ground, reducing the total supply of one of the world's most precious resources.
   Rhetorical Purpose:_____
   _____
   _____

3. America's precious wetlands are inhabited by numerous plant and animal species, which need to be preserved to maintain biological diversity.
   Rhetorical Purpose:_____
   _____
   _____

### Exercise 5

For each of the following sentences, identify the rhetorical purpose from list on previous page. Next, convert passive to active voice or leave passive voice if it fulfills a rhetorical purpose.

1. Research will be presented by senior psychology majors at the conference.
2. The students' proposal to leave early for the holidays is being considered by the dean and her staff.
3. Care packages for troops were arranged by freshmen students.
4. To save time, the research paper was written on a library computer.
5. Police are being notified that three prisoners have escaped.
6. The newest stock for the clothing store was inventoried by several part-time employees.
7. Surgeons successfully performed a new experimental liver-transplant operation.
8. A new experimental liver-transplant operation was performed successfully by the surgeons.

*What is the "Flesch-Kincaid Grade Level"—as shown in the "Readability Statics" lowest section?*

This scale, developed by Flesch and J. Peter Kincaid, an educator and scientist in the mid-1970s, aimed to demonstrate

- readability levels for Department of Defense/military documents and manuals. Since the early 1980s, the F–K grade
- level formula is used in educational reading levels for textbooks, K–12. Later with the introduction of word-processing
- programs, the range extended into the undergraduate and graduate levels.

Accordingly, the range is K–17 with, for example, a 7.6 grade level for a seventh-grade science textbook meaning "seven years, six months." Though "Grade 13" equates to a first-year college level, a common target range for early college writing is levels eleven

**Table 7.4   Examples of Reading Ease**

| Reading Ease | Level of Comprehension | Example of Publications | Purposeful Reading |
|---|---|---|---|
| 80–100 | Average eleven-year-old student | *Hunger Games* by Suzanne Collins | Pleasure Reading |
| 60–70 | Thirteen to fifteen-year-old students | *Readers Digest; Time* magazine | Close Reading |
| 40–60 | College students | *Wall Street Journal; The Economist* | Closer Reading |
| 0–30 | College graduates | *Journal of Animal Science; Yale Journal of International Law* | Closest Reading |

and twelve. The FS grade level is based on word count, not word order; and a writer still needs to consider purpose, audience, tone, and meanings of words.

*What is the Flesch Reading Ease Score?*

This scale, developed by author Rudolf Flesch in 1949, ranges between zero and 100. The lower the number (e.g., thirty), the more difficult the reading. The simplicity or complexity of reading are both based on words per-sentence and syllables-per-words. (An average sentence length for comfortable reading is twenty words.) A common target range for the general population is sixty to seventy.

*How do writers decrease the reading ease and increase grade level?*

1. Convert monosyllabic (one syllable) to polysyllabic (two or more syllables) words
2. Combine short sentences into more complex sentences
3. Increase average sentence length
4. Reduce passive voice

*How is passive and active voice related to reading?* A reader's background knowledge, purpose, understanding of vocabulary, and interest in the topic all influence "readability," that is, the ease or difficulty of the text. A reader's purpose may be one or more of the following:

- Enjoyment
- Skimming (reading for main idea or understanding; not reading every word)
- Scanning (looking for a word, fact, or detail; gain specific knowledge; not reading every word)
- Close reading (understanding and analysis)
- Reflective reading (application, synthesis, and evaluation)—specific words—often proper nouns.

*Linking Verbs*

Linking verbs are bridges that join words surrounding them. In other words, they are connectors of the subject to information about the subject. This information comes in the form of a subject complement—a noun, pronoun, or adjective that refers to the subject. Linking verbs do not express action, which explains why they are always present in passive voice.

***Example 4***
*Common linking verbs in the subject-verb-subject complement (S-LV-SC) sentence pattern:*

John Kerry is secretary of state. The fourth-grade students were tired.

**Table 7.5   Action Verbs**

| Action Verbs | | | | | |
|---|---|---|---|---|---|
| Accomplished | Classified | Documented | Gained | Installed | Questioned |
| Achieved | Clarified | Dodged | Gambled | Instilled | Received |
| Answered | Completed | Employed | Generated | Justified | Recommended |
| Anticipated | Commissioned | Encouraged | Governed | Located | Referred |
| Approved | Conceived | Engineered | Guarded | Managed | Responded |
| Assimilated | Conceptualized | Enlarged | Hired | Mastered | Researched |
| Augmented | Constructed | Examined | Handled | Observed | Saved |
| Advocated | Counseled | Established | Helped | Obtained | Selected |
| Believed | Created | Expressed | Hunted | Operated | Served |
| Bewildered | Demonstrated | Facilitated | Hypothesized | Participated | Shaped |
| Bloomed | Developed | Financed | Illustrated | Perceived | Structured |
| Boosted | Devised | Formatted | Implemented | Planned | Trained |
| Bounced | Diagnosed | Formulated | Improvised | Proposed | Transformed |
| Brushed | Displayed | Furnished | Inspected | Projected | Utilized |

**Table 7.6  Linking and "To Be" Verbs**

| Common Linking and "To Be" Verbs | | |
|---|---|---|
| *Common Linking Verbs* | | *"To Be" Verbs* |
| Am | Has | Am |
| Are | Have | Are |
| Be | Is | Be |
| Been | May | Being |
| Being | Might | Been |
| Can | Must | Is |
| Could | Shall | Was |
| Did | Should | Were |
| Do | Was | *Considered weakest verbs since they express no action nor value on their own. |
| Does | Were | |
| Had | Will | |
| | Would | |
| *Other Linking Verbs* | | *Sensory Linking Verbs* |
| Appear | | Feel |
| Get | | Look |
| Grow | | Smell |
| Look | | Sound |
| Prove | | Taste |
| Remain | | *Used when no action is present in sentences |
| Stay | | |

### Example 5
*Other linking verbs in the S-LV-SC sentence pattern:*

Students stayed for Biology tutoring sessions. The biology exam proved difficult for the class.

### Example 6
*Examples of sensory linking verbs in the S-LV-SC sentence pattern:*

The blackberry cobbler tasted delicious. The piano sounded out of tune.

## IMPROVING COHERENCE IN WRITING: GIVEN-NEW METHOD

### Essentials

*What is the role of a writer regarding coherence or linking ideas together for their readers?* As a writer, your role is that of a tour guide taking your audience through your thoughts and ideas, while steering clear of repetition and awkward phrases. As a guide, decide first how much your readers need to learn, refresh, or fill-in-the-blanks. This is an important decision because they will know you considered their familiarity (or lack of) with the topic. Linking ideas within or across paragraphs helps to improve the flow and coherence of writing.

*How can a writer create better coherence?* Writers can make their writing "cohere" better through (1) transition words or sentences; and (2) the Given-New (G-N) method. This approach is a "coherence check" to ensure your ideas link together and your writing has a nice rhythm. Smooth writing, by comparison, is like a rolling tide with a smooth ebb and flow.

The "Given-New" method works on the premise that every sentence contains content that is familiar and generally understood (given) and content that is unfamiliar or may not be understood (new) to the audience. Every word in every sentence is categorized as "given" or "new."

*How much given and new information does a writer include in every sentence, paragraph, or entire piece of writing?* The rhetorical strategy is a decision of how much given and new information to include in the writing. The answer is writing is always audience-driven. If audience wants to learn information, use less given and more new information. If audience's purposes are to learn and to refresh, use some given and some new information. If audience's purpose is to refresh, use more given and less new information.

Determining how much new and how much given information to include, think of the rhetorical situation that surrounds your writing. Back to the tour guide approach. Think of your audience: What do they need to know? How familiar are they with your topic? How much to keep their interest? Steer clear of boredom? Remind them of? Assume is understood?

*What is important to know about given and new information in introductory and concluding sentences?* Remember how your composition instructor said, "Don't put new information in a conclusion?" The reason is that, typically, the first sentence (or paragraph) contains "new" information, and the last sentence (or paragraph) contains "given" information. Within sentences, the "given" information is most often found at the beginning of the sentence, followed by the new information, which becomes the "given" information in the subsequent sentence. However, the given and new information can appear anywhere in subsequent sentences. "Given" information is sometimes implicitly understood by the audience who infer meaning or fill in the blanks.

First Paragraph in a Document:
Body Paragraph:
Concluding Paragraph:

## *Example 7*

## Student's Annotated Bibliography showing Given-New Method

*Italics* = "New" information
Underlined = "Given" information

Dahiya, Monica Balyan. "Quest for the past in an alien land: a study of Jhumpa Lahiri's Namesake and

**Table 7.7   Given-New Method, Part 1**

| First sentence: New (N) | | |
|---|---|---|
| Second sentence: Given (G) | → | (N) |
| Third sentence: Given (G) | → | (N) |
| Fourth sentence: Given (G) | → | (N) |
| Last sentence: (G) | | |

**Table 7.8   Given-New Method, Part 2**

| First sentence: Given (G) and New (N) | | |
|---|---|---|
| Second sentence: (G) | → | (N) |
| Third sentence: (G) | → | (N) |
| Fourth sentence: (G) | → | (N) |
| Last sentence: (G) | | |

**Table 7.9   Given-New Method, Part 3**

| First sentence: Given (G) |
|---|
| Second sentence: Given (G) |
| Third sentence: Given (G) |
| Fourth sentence: Given (G) |

Bharati Mukherjee's Jasmine." *Language in India* July 2012: 497+. Literature Resource Center. Web. 29 September 2014.

*The essay by Monica Balyan Dahiya is a secondary source because the essay is an opinionated piece and does not provide any factual contents.* The *main purpose* of this essay *is to "draw immigrants back to their roots and analyze the causes and consequences of alienation"* (2). Monica Balyan Dahiya interprets *why many* aliens *who settle in different countries take a piece of* their *culture back with them.* She conveys how the aliens *assimilate with their own culture while* they *balance the cultivation of the place* they *are residing.* She emphasizes *different examples* of alienation and the *emotions of* immigrants. She begins with *"roots"* as one of her examples and states that *"[g]eographical displacement rarely makes an* immigrant *fail to remember emotional bonding with native land or original home"* (3). Dahiya explains alienation in *depth* by using specific examples from The Namesake *with the characters Ashima, Gogol, and Sonia to help prove her point* about immigrants settling in a new land. She describes alienation as *"one of the significant ingredients that indicate an* immigrant's *transportation, exile, uprooting and sense of loneliness in a new atmosphere"* (3). Dahiya conveys this point by stating that Ashima's alienation is contributed by her *observance two conflicting cultures* and the way Sonia and Gogol are *raised.* When Gogol and Sonia *are introduced to different Indian practices,* they are confused at first because they are not born into a *fully embraced Indian culture like* Ashima. Dahiya goes into a concept called *"The Second Generation"* which *explicates how the children of the first generation have a better chance at a more successful life than that of their parents (4).* She states, "The second generation lives a better life than the parents whose roots still do not allow them to embrace the foreign land but their *identity always reflects* their parents past migrant history" which is *true* in Gogol and Sonia's case (4). She explains how the parents of the second generation children want them to *succeed and follow the American dream,* but at the same time, *follow the culture embedded* in their parents. This essay is a great source because the arguments focus greatly on the blending of two cultures and focuses on immigrants and specifically to the immigrants in The Namesake.

## *Exercise 6*

Using two colors or the italics and underline functions, label "Given-New" information in the following article: "The Birth of Mount Rushmore":

Mount Rushmore, located just north of Custer State Park in South Dakota's Black Hills National Forest, was named for the New York lawyer Charles E. Rushmore, who traveled to the Black Hills in 1884 to inspect mining claims in the region. When Rushmore asked a local man the name of a nearby mountain, he reportedly replied that it never had a name before, but from now on would be known as Rushmore Peak (later Rushmore Mountain or Mount Rushmore).

A bill introduced in Congress in 1937 proposed that a carving of Susan B. Anthony's head be included among the luminaries at Mount Rushmore, but fell through due to a rider on the existing appropriations bill mandating that federal funds be spent only on those carvings already begun. Seeking to attract tourism to the Black Hills in the early 1920s, South Dakota's state historian Doane Robinson came up with the idea to sculpt "the Needles" (several giant natural granite pillars) into the shape of historic heroes of the West.

He suggested Red Cloud, a Sioux chief, as a potential subject. In August 1924, Robinson contacted Gutzon Borglum, an American sculptor of Danish descent who was then working on carving an image of the Confederate General Robert E. Lee into the face of Georgia's Stone Mountain. Luckily for Robinson, the headstrong Borglum was on the outs with the group that had commissioned the Lee sculpture and would soon abandon the project. Borglum suggested that the subjects of the South Dakota work be George Washington and Abraham Lincoln, as that would attract more national interest. He would later add Thomas Jefferson and Theodore Roosevelt to the list, in recognition of their contributions to the birth of democracy and the growth of the United States ("The Birth of Mount Rushmore").

## CHOOSING EXACT WORDS

### Essentials

*Why it is important for writers to use exact words (proper nouns)?* Using more exact words referring to particular people, places, and things enriches writing for readers. More specific words evoke readers' visual sense, which helps them to engage in your writing. The easiest way to explain this is to use more proper—rather than common—nouns.

The rule-of-thumb is the more capital letters, the more specific the words. For instance, instead of author, Stephen King; instead of country, Indonesia; instead of search engine, Google; instead of road,

**Table 7.10  Common and Proper Nouns**

| Common Nouns | Proper Nouns |
| --- | --- |
| Does not name person, place, nor thing | Names person, place, or thing |
| Generic | Specific |
| Not capitalized | Capitalized |

Rt. 66; instead of fruit, Georgia peaches. You get the idea! General nouns such as "society, community, world, and thing" create vague, general writing.

### Example 8

General: The voters completed their ballots.
Specific: The 9th district voters completed their state of Louisiana ballots carefully.
General: There are regional dialects spoken in the country.
Specific: At least six distinct regional dialects, such as the Midwest and Southeast, are spoken in the United States.

### Exercise 7
In the following paragraph, underline the proper nouns that help you to picture the scene that Michael Crichton created in *Jurassic Park*:

Such a new and distinctive pattern led [an American biologist living in Costa Rica, Dr. Martin "Marty"] Guitierrez to suspect the presence of a previously unknown species of lizard. This was particularly likely to happen in Cost Rica. Only seventy-five miles wide at the narrowest point, the country was smaller than the state of Maine. Yet, within its limited space, Costa Rica had a remarkable diversity of biological habitats: seacoasts on both the Atlantic and the Pacific; four separate mountain ranges including twelve-thousand-foot peaks and active volcanoes; rain forests; cloud forests, temperate zones, swampy marshes, and arid deserts. Such ecological diversity sustained an astonishing diversity of plant and animal life. Costa Rica had three times as many species of birds as all of North America. More than a thousand species of orchids. More than five thousand species of insects.

### Exercise 8
In the blank beside each common noun, write examples of a proper noun. Then use proper nouns in sentences.

For example, Country: Northern Ireland. Specific Nouns: We visited Northern Ireland's Giant's

Causeway, sheep farms, St. Patrick's Centre, and local "Bangers and Mash" restaurants.

### *Exercise 9*

1. Game_____
2. It _____
3. Society _____
4. Thing _____

### *Exercise 10*

In the blank spaces, insert transition words that improve coherence and clarity. (In most cases, there were no transition words in the original text.

National Geographic, "Earth."

Earth, our home planet, is the only planet in our solar system known to harbor life. All of the things we need to survive are provided under a thin layer of atmosphere that separates us from the uninhabitable void of space. [ ], Earth is made up of complex, interactive systems that are often unpredictable. Air, water, land, and life—including humans—combine forces to create a constantly changing world that we are striving to understand.

[ ] viewing Earth from the unique perspective of space provides the opportunity to see Earth as a whole. Scientists around the world have discovered many things about our planet by working together and sharing their findings.

Some facts are well known. [ ], Earth is the third planet from the sun and the fifth largest in the solar system. Earth's diameter is just a few hundred kilometers larger than that of Venus. [ ], the four seasons are a result of Earth's axis of rotation being tilted more than 23 degrees.

Oceans at least 2.5 miles (4 kilometers) deep cover nearly 70 percent of Earth›s surface. Fresh water exists in the liquid phase only within a narrow temperature span (32 to 212 degrees Fahrenheit/0 to 100 degrees Celsius).

[ ], this temperature span is especially narrow when contrasted with the full range of temperatures found within the solar system. [ ], the presence and distribution of water vapor in the atmosphere is responsible for much of Earth's weather. 82 science.nationalgeographic.com/science/space/solar-system/earth.

**Table 7.11  Transitional Words and Phrases**

**Transitional Words and Phrases**

| *To Add Information* | *To Compare/Contrast* | *To Draw Conclusions* |
|---|---|---|
| Additionally | But | As a result |
| Also | By comparison | Consequently |
| And | Comparatively | For these reasons |
| Concurrently | Conversely | It follows that |
| Equally important | However | Since |
| Furthermore | In contrast | Therefore |
| In addition | Likewise | The final outcome… |
| Increasingly important | Nevertheless | Thus |
| Likewise | Paralleling | To complete |
| Moreover | Similar to… or Similarly | To finalize |
| Too | Yet | Unquestionably |

| *To Explain* | *To Illustrate* | *To Qualify* |
|---|---|---|
| As a matter of fact | For example | Although |
| Accordingly | For instance | Assuredly |
| Besides | Incidentally | Frequently |
| Especially | In this case | In fact |
| Evidently | More specifically | In particular |
| Furthermore | Namely | In spite of this |
| Indeed | Take for example | Gradually |
| Notably | To clarify | Meanwhile |
| Of major interest | To demonstrate | Most of all |
| That is or That is to say | To illustrate | Under these circumstances |
| That is why… | To show… | Without exception |

| *To Repeat* | *To Show Time and Sequence* | *To Summarize* |
|---|---|---|
| As stated | Afterwards | As noted |
| As noted | Currently | Cumulatively |
| By way of recall | Earlier | In brief |
| In other words | Finally | A summation of… |
| In retrospect | First, Secondly, Third, etc. | Finally |
| To recount | Immediately | Lastly |
| To recapitulate | Initially | Overall |
| To reconsider To reexamine | Next | Therefore |
| To review | Prior to | To recapitulate |
| To reevaluate | Still | To summarize |
|  | Subsequently | Up to this point |

*Chapter 8*

# Documenting Sources

## ESSENTIALS

To begin, a note on plagiarism:

Preventing plagiarism in academia continues to require respect for intellectual property, careful scholarship, and a strong personal code of honor. Plagiarism, whether intentional or unintentional, for monetary gain or other benefit, is academia's most serious offense. In academic plagiarism, the only one hurt is the plagiarist, who trades long-term honor for short-term convenience or the hope of good grades.

The concept of plagiarism is not a modern invention; rather, it has a history nearly as long as that of the written word. The term *plagiarism*, according to the *Oxford English Dictionary* (*OED*), was coined by the ancient Roman poet Martial from the Latin *plagiarius*, "one who abducts a child or slave of another." Thus, a *plagiarius* would be a sort of literary kidnapper. In Martial's case, his verses—his "child"—were stolen and circulated as the property of another.

In more recent times, electronic media, photographic reproduction, the personal computer, and the Internet added new dimensions to the old problem of plagiarism. In academia, few college professors or disciplinary boards consider intention when assessing blame: the final written product looks the same regardless of the author's intention. In the end, writers are responsible for the work they hand in as their own. Putting one's name on an article, research paper, or homework assignment establishes the writer's intention of claiming credit for everything not specifically credited to someone else. Avoiding plagiarism requires diligent self-inspection and the determination to learn good study habits and research methods—the same habits of mind which help internalize honor codes present at colleges and universities.

(Dr. Faye Ringel, "Correct Paraphrase and Documentation:

How to Avoid Plagiarism the Honor Offense for Academics")

*Why is there such a big emphasis on the exact format of citation?* Just as the application of the ethics of citation is rigorous in all academic disciplines, so too is the application of the rules governing the format of citation. It will be your responsibility to enter the academic conversation in each discipline you study, to determine which style of citation will be required for writing in science and technology, social science, and humanities courses. The presentation of research is fundamental in higher education, and you will become part of that ongoing process.

*What is the key to avoiding plagiarism?* The key is documenting sources accurately. The three primary reasons for documentation are: providing support to your argument in order to persuade your audience that your reasoning is sound and credible; enabling the audience to trace your sources should they want to read and/or validate them as credible and useful; and "giving credit where credit is due" to pay respect to the intellectual property of writers. All three reasons reflect your intrinsic ethos and appeal to extrinsic ethos—to the character and ethics of the audience.

*How does a writer document sources according to standardized style manuals?* Style manuals provide rules for citing any type of information. Examples of style manuals include *American Chemical Society* (ACS), *American Psychological Association* (APA), *Chicago Documentation Style: Elements* (CDS or CMS) or *Turabian* (T), *Council of Science Editors* (CSE), and *Modern Language Association* (MLA). Use the style appropriate to the discipline:

MLA—English and history; APA—psychology, sociology, education, and zoology; CDS—political science; and CSE—biology and physics; and ACS—chemistry. Since this work text is primarily for English courses, the emphasized style is MLA.

Note: Three methods of documenting sources: quoting, paraphrasing, and summarizing. What is considered "common knowledge" does not require documentation. All four of these topics will be discussed later in this chapter.

*What are the features of a scholarly source?*

- appears in reputable publications
- bibliography
- cites credible sources
- clear primary audience
- found in online databases and library stacks
- higher-level vocabulary
- nonprofit
- peer reviews necessary for selection of articles
- presents research findings
- specialized academic style

### Example 1
*College Composition and Communication, Scientific American, Aeronautics and Aerospace Engineering, Political Science Quarterly*, and *Harvard Business Review.*

*What is a periodical—root word: "periodic"?*

- issued at regular intervals; examples: biweekly, monthly, annually
- journals, magazines, and newspapers

### Example 2
*Washington Post, Time, Newsweek, San Francisco Chronicle, Journal of Law and Conflict Resolution*, and *International Journal of Fisheries and Aquaculture.*

*What is important to remember when selecting sources?*

- Cite from full text documents (print analogs), not abstracts. Citing an abstract is similar to reading a film review without watching the film. Use print analogs—dictionaries, journals, and newspapers, which are all printed in full text and usually require subscription for access.
- Draw from .edu, .gov, .mil, or org. sites, which are regulated and typically require peer reviews to affirm the publications are credible. Examples of websites: *owl.english.purdue.edu; energy.gov;*

*usa4militaryfamilies.dod.mil*; and *NPR. org*. When possible, steer away from .com sites as they are commercially based, that is, driven by advertising to attract customers, exhibit heavy bias (the sponsoring company is often the author). Some .com sites are credible, but most exhibit features described above.

- Select sources from within the past five years (ideally) or ten years (realistically). The more current the sources, the more reliable your research projects.
- Choose databases supported by your school or local library because those databases reflect scholarship. For example, *ProQuest, Expanded Academic Index, LexisNexis Academic,* and *InfoTrac.*
- When searching for a site, remember Boolean search commands: X or Y (expands); X and Y (narrows); X not Y (limits).
- When choosing sources, favor primary rather than secondary texts.
- When selecting an article or other text, look for accuracy, authority, coverage, currency, format, and objectivity.
- When deciding if a website is credible or not, look up the site on behinddomain.org
- Use credible—open and free—databases: Internet Public Library (www.ipl.org), Library of Congress (www.catalog.loc.gov), and Martindale's The Reference Desk (www.martindalecenter.com).
- The most applicable encyclopedia for secondary and college students is *Encyclopedia Britannica* (www.britannica. com), and the most applicable dictionary is *Oxford English Dictionary* (www.oed .com). Both require subscriptions. Check to see if your library subscribes to these sites.

*What is the difference between a "Works Cited" section and a "Works Consulted" section?* A Works Cited section is a section containing the bibliography or reference list of sources cited directly by the writer.

A Works Consulted section is a section containing the bibliography or reference list of sources not cited directly by the writer; the writer has only consulted these sources for background knowledge/research purposes. A Works Consulted section broadly informs the writer's thinking; therefore, it still requires acknowledgment in a presentation at the end of a piece of writing. Check with your instructor to determine if both Works Cited and Works Consulted are required.

## PRIMARY AND SECONDARY SOURCES

### Essentials

*What is the main difference between a primary and a secondary source?* A primary source is an original text, whereas a secondary source is not an original text. A secondary source is a writer's comments or analysis of a primary source.

*What is the value of a primary source?* Primary sources are the preservation of the past. Human memory and storytelling across generations are the only other forms of preserving the past. This proves invaluable when we have direct access to documents—unfiltered and precise. Primary sources have an authenticity not necessarily present in secondary sources. For instance, research conducted by writers in the sciences and technology and published in scholarly journals (or other) is primary-source material. Journalists who analyze and popularize research presented in newspapers and magazines offer us secondary sources. When selecting sources, always opt for as many primary sources as possible so as to form the impression that you are a motivated researcher with high standards for your work. When

**Table 8.1   Primary and Secondary Sources**

| *Primary Sources* | *Secondary Sources* |
| --- | --- |
| Almanac | Biography |
| Artifact | Commentary |
| Atlas | Course textbook |
| Autobiography/Memoir | Critical review |
| Certificate: birth, marriage; diploma | Dictionary |
| Diary or personal journal | Encyclopedia |
| Editorial | Historical account or recount |
| Film/Documentary | Newspaper or magazine articles (with exceptions) |
| Green card | |
| Interview | |
| Letter | |
| Narratives | |
| Novel | |
| Oral history | |
| Photograph | |
| Play | |
| Poem | |
| Publication by expert: article, book, column. | |
| Research study/findings | |
| Sermon | |
| Short Story | |
| Speech | |
| Testimonial | |
| U.S. Census Data | |
| Video recording | |

| *Examples of Primary Sources* | *Examples of Secondary Sources* |
| --- | --- |
| • Alexander Hamilton, one author of the *Federalist Papers* | • Newspaper article in *Denver Post* on a car accident |
| • Charles Dicken's original manuscript for *Tale of Two Cities* | • *Environmental Science* by Eldon Enger and Bradley Smith (February 18, 2009) |
| • Jonathan Edwards' *Sinners in the Hands of an Angry God* | • *Room Full of Mirrors: A Biography of Jimi Hendrix* by Charles R. Cross |
| • National Geographic's documentary: *Grand Canyon: The Hidden Secrets* | • *Oxford English Dictionary* |
| • *The Complete Collected Poems of Maya Angelou* | • Schultz, Norman. "Historical Facts." *Beyond Intractability.* Eds. Guy Burgess and Heidi Burgess. Conflict Information Consortium, University of Colorado, Boulder |
| • *Margaret Thatcher: The Autobiography* by Margaret Thatcher | • *Margaret Thatcher: From Grantham to the Falklands* by Charles Moore |
| • *The Letters of J.R.R. Tolkien* | • "Fatal car accident on New Jersey Turnpike," Reena Rose Sibayan/*The Jersey Journal*, July 10, 2014 |
| • "Accident sends car crashing into house in Paterson, NJ" | |
| • WABC News, New York (video clip), July 27, 2014 | |
| • Film review on RottenTomatoes.com | |

reading primary sources, read slowly. They are filled with dense information and require critical reading to comprehend their theses and evidence.

### Exercise 1
Are the following texts scholarly or nonscholarly?

_____ "Is criminal behavior a central component of psychopathy? Conceptual directions for resolving the debate" by Jennifer Skeem and David J. Cooke in *Psychological Assessment* journal

_____ *Einstein: His Life and Universe* by Walter Isaacson

_____ *Rocket Girl: The Story of Mary Sherman Morgan, America's First Female Rocket Scientist* by George D. Morgan

_____ *Time* magazine article

_____ *Tampa Bay Times* newspaper

_____ *GQ* magazine

### Exercise 2
Are the following primary or secondary texts, or both?

_____ *War Letters* by Andrew Carroll (collection of authentic letters written to and from soldiers and their loved ones during Civil–Persian Gulf Wars).

_____ *World Religions: Origins History Practices Beliefs Worldview* by Franjo Terhart and Janina Schulze, writers and scholars of religion.

_____ *A Collection of Sermons Given in Paris c. 1267, Including a New Text by Saint Bonaventura on the Life of Saint Francis* by Robert E. Lerner who offers commentary about the sermons and provides digitized copies of the original sermons.

_____ "College students' prevalence and perceptions of text messaging while driving" by Marissa Harrison who reports the findings of her study in *Accident Analysis & Prevention* journal.

_____ "Sun and Wind Alter Global Landscape, Leaving Utilities Behind" by Justin Gillis, who reports on the topic in *The New York Times*.

_____ *Amazing Grace*—a film based on true events featuring William Wilberforce, an English politician who seeks to abolish slavery in Britain in the face of major opposition in the 1700s.

_____ *Beowulf: A Translation and Commentary* by Christopher Tolkien and J. R. R. Tolkien.

## CITING SOURCES: QUOTING, PARAPHRASING, AND SYNTHESIZING

### Essentials

*Why is citing sources a critical part of writing and research?* Citing sources is an important and necessary part of writing essays that require supporting evidence. Since many topics have been researched in the past, think of a research assignment as continuing a conversation rather than starting one. You can add some valuable thoughts to this conversation while establishing your own intrinsic ethos in the process. By documenting sources, you are giving credit to the intellectual properties of authors on whose shoulders you stand. Paying respect to these rights requires attention to detail when paraphrasing, quoting, and summarizing source content.

*What are the fundamental differences among quotations, paraphrases, and summaries?* (See Table 8.2)

*When do you quote vs. paraphrase vs. summarize?* The answer lies in your purpose and source. Consider these questions:

### Quoting

By definition, a "quotation" is a reproduction of the author's exact words with no alterations.

*What are the features of a quotation?*

**Table 8.2   Documenting Sources**

| Citations | Author's Words? | Author's Meaning? | Your Words? | Your Meaning? |
| --- | --- | --- | --- | --- |
| Quotations | Yes | Yes | No | No |
| Paraphrases | No | Yes | Yes | No |
| Summaries | No | Yes | Yes | Yes & No |

**Table 8.3  Questions About Documenting Sources**

| Questions | Yes? | No? |
|---|---|---|
| Are the author's words expressed better verbatim? | Quote | Paraphrase |
| Are the author's words memorable and sacred "as is"? | Quote | Paraphrase |
| Is "less, more"? Can you state the author's meaning in a concise way? | Paraphrase | Quote |
| Do you need only to state main points? | Summarize | Quote or Paraphrase |

- Citation
- Single quotes within double quotes
- Ellipses and/or brackets to indicate missing words
- Quote marks around author's original words (verbatim)

*What should you consider when selecting a quotation?*

- The quotation should add value to the evidence in support of the topic sentence
- The quotation should contain enough context for understanding; author's meaning should not be misrepresented
- The quotation should contain a memorable or significant point

*How much text is included in a block quotation?* The rule-of-thumb is that four or more lines require a block quote.

*What are the features of a block quotation, MLA style?*

- No quotation marks
- Indented ten spaces from left margin
- Double-space above and below the quotation
- Introduced with signal phrase

Here is an example of a block quotation.
A representative explained,

On the eve of Memorial Day, thousands of people descend on the mall in Washington D.C. to listen to American musicians pay tribute to the men and women in uniform. This is an annual tradition in which members from all branches of the military and their loved ones receive deserved praise for the sacrifices they make for our country. (46)

*What are the features of an indirect quotation?*

- Reporting someone's words, but not exactly or verbatim

- No quotation marks
- Include the word "that" prior to quotation

Indirect Quotation: Kathleen said that the car needed an oil change. Direct Quotation: Kathleen said, "The car needs an oil change."
*What are the features of a quotation within a quotation?*

- Different voice speaking within a quotation
- Single quotation marks around the quotation within a quotation

Suzanne told her coach, "I'm sorry I missed practice, but I would still like to play in our game this Saturday. According to our player manual, 'If a student misses practice due to a medical reason, the coach must assess the condition to play in upcoming games,' and I had the flu."

*What is problematic about quoting out of context?* Treating others' words with respect encompasses more than giving credit to the author: you must understand the author's argument before relying upon it to support yours. To "quote out of context" means that the writer or speaker—accidentally or deliberately—uses another's words inaccurately. This practice distorts the meaning of the quoted words, by supporting a different conclusion than the one intended.

### Example 3
The movie industry is notorious for deliberately choosing certain favorable words from a review and featuring them in advertisements, although the original review may have been unfavorable. According to an article in *Slate*, "'[Best] Film Ever!!!': How do movie blurbs work?"

*Entertainment Weekly* gave the 1995 film *Se7en* a "B" grade. . . . The critic praised the film's introductory credits sequence as "a small masterpiece of dementia." But the newspaper ads ran a banner that simply said, "A Masterpiece," as if the critic had been referring to the whole film. (Beam)

**Table 8.4   Signal Words**

| Signal Words | |
| --- | --- |
| Acknowledges | Emphasizes |
| Adds | Grants |
| Admits | Illustrates |
| Agrees | Implies |
| Argues | Insists |
| Asserts | Notes |
| Believes | Observes |
| Claims | Points out |
| Comments | Reasons that |
| Compares | Refutes |
| Confirms | Rejects |
| Contends | Reports |
| Declares | Responds |
| Denies | Suggests |
| Disputes | Thinks |
| Endorses | Writes |

Politicians are also known for changing the meaning of their opponents' words by quoting them out of context. In the 2012 presidential campaign, Republican candidate Mitt Romney was accused of being a heartless CEO who bought companies and laid off their employees. In the original rhetorical situation, Romney was answering a question about health care policies at a meeting in New Hampshire. Endorsing a free market in health-care providers, he responded, "'I like being able to fire people who provide services to me.' . . . 'If someone doesn't give me a good service that I need, I want to say, 'I'm going to go get someone else to provide that service to me.''" (qtd. in Madison and Boxer). The video clip of the candidate saying "I like being able to fire people" appeared in commercials next to footage of unemployed workers. This, too, constitutes quoting out of context.

College students are less likely to quote deliberately out of context; rather, they may misinterpret a source or attribute an opinion to a writer who is actually arguing against that opinion. The result is still a distortion of the original writer's words, even if quoted and documented correctly.

### *Example 4*

A passage and a student's mistaken attribution follows:

*Original*

From: Alfie Kohn, "The Schools Our Children Deserve: Moving Beyond Traditional Classrooms and Tougher Standards"

Some may fear that students will be unsuccessful in life if they haven't been graded or if those grades aren't impressive. According to recent research,

however, he argues that "students who are given grades. . . tend to (1) display less interest in what they are doing, (2) fare worse on meaningful measures of learning, and (3) avoid more difficult tasks when given the opportunity." Therefore, he concludes, "whether we are concerned about love of learning, quality of thinking, or preference for challenge, students lucky enough to attend schools that do not give letter or number grades fare better . . . The more they can forget about grades, the better the chances they will be engaged with ideas.

Student Paraphrase:

Alfie Kohn once wrote on the topic of traditional grading standards and how they could be improved. He argued "students will not be successful in life if they have not been graded or if those grades aren't impressive."

Here, even though the student has placed the quoted words within quotation marks and has acknowledged the source, the result is still a bad paraphrase, since the words have been quoted out of context. Eliminating the original words "some may fear" makes it seem as though Kohn believes these fears are well-founded. Instead, he argues against those who hold this view.

*Common Knowledge*

*What are the features of common knowledge?*

- Audience-driven
- Found in reference texts: encyclopedias, dictionaries, almanacs, and collections
- Information recognizable by an average, educated reader
- Not cited
- Verified in three or more credible sources

*Note*: Document any informational text—visual or written—that is not your own. If in doubt whether a piece of information (e.g., signing of the Declaration of Independence in 1776) is common knowledge, document the source.

### Paraphrasing

*What is a paraphrase?* By definition, to "paraphrase" is to use your own words in a piece of writing to express another author's meaning.

*What are the features of a paraphrase?*

1. Cited
2. Changed sentence structure and rhythm

3. Different words and phrases
4. Loyal to writer's meaning
5. Key points
6. Shorter than original

*Note*: A paraphrase does not attempt to recreate the full effect of the author's writing; instead, a paraphrase tries to map out the key ideas and meaning.

*What are the features of selected text to paraphrase?*

- At minimum, three or four sentences
- Avoids highly specialized vocabulary
- Contains assertions or opinions, not only facts
- Information-dense
- Minimal to no numerical data (words lend themselves more easily to paraphrasing)

*Which texts should a writer avoid paraphrasing?*

- Fiction: drama, poetry, and short stories (sacred and masterful writing left alone)
- Numerical data and statistics

## Patchwriting

*What is patchwriting?* Patchwriting is a subcategory of paraphrasing. By definition, patchwriting is mimicking an author's syntax while "patching" your words (i.e., synonyms) intermittently onto the author's writing. The outcome is a mixture of your words and your sources, while retaining the source's syntax. An unacceptable form of paraphrasing, patch writing is a lazy form of documenting a source. Patch writing falls between original text and a true paraphrase:

Original text > Patch writing > Paraphrasing

## Music Sampling and Paraphrasing

*What is "Music Sampling"?* Music sampling is using a part—beats, bass line, vocals, pitch, other instruments, or even a microsecond of background noise— of a musician's song. For example, a few bars containing a drum beat repeat in "looped" sequence to form the backbeat of the new recording. Samples are manipulated in different ways and combined with other sounds and sound effects to make a new version of a song or recording. Music sampling requires permission; otherwise, the result is copyright violation of the audio portion and the song itself. The use of sound recording; any substantial use without permission constitutes infringement; "heart of song" must be recognizable.

*How is music sampling related to paraphrasing?* Both require adhering to principles requiring giving credit where credit is due.

*In brief, what is the history of music sampling?* An early song utilizing music sampling was on a hip-hop record—a hired band to record a copy of "Good Times," then rapped over the lyrics, which resulted in song: "Rapper's Delight." In 1989, a band 2 Live Crew sampled Roy Orbison's "Pretty Woman" song, using the same name of the song and altering some lyrics. This resulted in legal infringement. In the early 1990s, Vanilla Ice (Robert Van Winkle) sampled the bassline of Queen and David Bowie's 1981 song, "Ice Ice Baby." He argued that he had added an additional note. Both sides argued in court and then settled. Van Winkle paid Queen and Bowie. Since then, a concept called "willful infringement" is now legal infringement in music sampling cases.

*What are several examples of legal music sampling?*

- Will Smith's "Men In Black" sampled part of the chorus from Patrice Rushen's "Forget Me Nots"
- Mary J. Blige's "No More Drama" sampled instrumental from Barry De Vorzon and Perry Botkin, Jr's "Nadia's Theme"
- Rihanna's SOS sampled composition from Ed Cobb's (then) Soft Cell's "Tainted Love" *Source*: Lindenbaum, John. "Music Sampling and Copyright Law." April, 1999.

*What are the similarities and differences between paraphrasing and Music Sampling?*

Table 8.5  **Differences Between Paraphrasing and Music Sampling**

|  | Paraphrasing | Music Sampling |
|---|---|---|
| No. of Words | ≥ 3 words | ≥ 3 words |
| Rhythm | Different rhythm | Different riff/melody |
| Words/Lyrics | Writer's words | Singer's words |
| Syntax | Different syntax | May be same syntax |
| Respect to author | Cited | Payment and citation |

## Summarizing

*What is a summary?* By definition, "summary" refers to a writer using his/her words to write the main points of an author's text.

*What are the features of a summary?*

- Includes an attributive tag
- Cited
- Focuses on main and supporting points
- Restates main ideas in your words
- Appears shorter than original text (length determined by purpose)
- Uses transition words/phrases

*What else is important to know about summaries?* The best way to express your understanding of the central points of an article, chapter, or other type of nonfiction reading is to write a clear summary. A summary can become a process of discovery to better comprehend an article or other reading. Ask yourself: What are the main and supporting points of this text? Similar to sand running through your fingers leaving only the shells and pebbles, you'll sift the text to find central ideas, while leaving minor details behind. Your goal when writing a summary is to interpret and report information. A summary serves a different purpose than an analysis—one is not the substitute for the other.

Original
From: William F. Buckley's "Why Don't We Complain?"

I think the observable reluctance of the majority of Americans to assert themselves in minor matters is related to our increased sense of helplessness in an age of technology and centralized political and economic power. For generations, Americans who were too hot, or too cold, got up and did something about it. Now we call the plumber, or the electrician, or the furnace man. The habit of looking after our own needs obviously had something to do with the assertiveness that characterized the American family familiar to the readers of American literature. With the technification of life goes our direct responsibility for our material environment, and we are conditioned to adopt a position of helplessness not only as regards the broken air conditioner but also as regards the overheated train. It takes an expert to fix the former but not the latter; yet these distinctions, as we withdraw into helplessness, tend to fade away. (61)

Acceptable Student Paraphrase

Buckley claims that people rely increasingly on others to fix modern conveniences and technological problems. Due to this reliance, people have become less certain about their own abilities to change anything major and fall into habits of not asserting themselves for anything minor. He argues that people have become complacent with respect to situations both in and beyond their control. (61)

Unacceptable Student Patch writing:

Buckley believes the observable reluctance of many Americans to speak up is associated with our increased sense of helplessness when the Internet is highly visible and also more centralized with political and economical power (61).

### Example 5
Acceptable Student Summary of "Know it All: Can Wikipedia Conquer Expertise?" by Stacy Schiff (full article found in online Instructors Guide)

Though *Wikipedia* is a democratic and comprehensive site, it has both pros and cons in terms of its credibility. Schiff argues in her essay: "Know It All: Can Wikipedia Conquer Expertise?" that Wikipedia is available to all citizens—children to adults—who choose to post and/or locate information about diverse topics. These topics range from reggae music to the origin of pizza to wildlife in Alaska, and even more. Several positive aspects of the site include: accessibility, currency, and inclusivity. Conversely, some of the negative aspects include: unknown authorship, nonverifiable information, questionable facts, and editing mistakes. In comparison to the Encyclopedia Britannica, its older "sister," Wikipedia includes postings on innumerable topics in several hundred languages updated daily, even hourly, that meet general criteria (e.g., content already published in a source). Encyclopedia Britannica has offered entries subjected to vetting by academic experts, thus providing more reliable facts for researchers. Wikipedia is fast reaching the goal of its founder, Jimmy Wales, to become an accessible site for citizens globally in their own languages. With awareness of its pros and cons, everyone can use Wikipedia as a source of any information, but not for serious research.

Paraphrasing, Quoting, and Summarizing Text using MLA style: *Parenthetical*

Option 1: Delaying last name of author and page number(s) until after the quotation. For example, ". . . ." (Gonzalez 16).

Option 2: Introducing author's last name ahead of quote (called an *Attributive Tag*), but delaying page number(s) until after quotation.

Gonzalez explained, ". . ." (16).

*Quoting a Source Within a Source*

Lee argued, ". . ." (qtd. in Miller 17).

### *Exercise 3*
Paraphrasing

Select an article and follow these steps to write a paraphrase:

1. Using criteria above, choose "paraphrasable" text
2. Read text; reread for main points
3. Zero in on one or two main point(s) or paragraphs Create a mini outline of key points in paragraphs
4. Look away from the text; mentally form a paraphrase that captures the writer's meaning
5. Change the sequence, thereby the rhythm, of the original words/sentences
6. Go down in meaning, not up
7. Cite the author (and, if available, page no.)

### *Exercise 4*
Summarizing

Select an article and follow these steps to write a summary:

1. Survey title, author, length, context, and topic sentences of each paragraph
2. Read and reread passage
3. Break passage into sections
4. Highlight key points and subpoints
5. Identify the writer's purpose, audience, and thesis
6. Write a thesis (your words) about passage
7. Write list of key points and subpoints
8. Write first draft of summary combining thesis and points
9. Eliminate any excess information, especially minor details
10. Cross reference your summary with passage and make adjustments as necessary
11. Rewrite your summary by inserting transitional words/phrases
12. Ask a friend to read for clarity and coherence; revise as necessary

### *Exercise 5*
Paraphrasing and Quoting

Read the following article and evaluate paraphrases in Versions 1-7

Boylanda, Emma J., et al. "Beyond-brand effect of television (TV) food advertisements/ commercials on caloric intake and food choice of five- to seven-year-old children." *Science Direct* 49.1 (2007): 263–67. Print.

A study by Emma J. Boylanda, et al. finds that "food advert[isement] exposure has been shown to influence caloric intake and food choice in 9–11 year olds. However, little is known about the effect of food advertisements on feeding behaviour in younger children. Therefore, [they] conducted a study with 93 children aged 5–7 years, 28 of whom were overweight or obese. The children were exposed to 10 non-food advert[isements] and 10 food advert[isements] in a repeated measures design. Their consumption of sweet and savoury, high- and low-fat snack foods, and fruit were measured following both sessions. Food advert[isement] exposure produced a significant increase in total food intake in young children . . . . Beyond their effects on brand choice, exposure to food advertisements (commercials) promotes over-consumption in younger children." (263–265)

Below are examples of documenting (quoting and paraphrasing) the original source (above). Imagine that you are an English instructor who evaluates versions in students' essays. Write: "correct" or "incorrect" documentation. Explain.

## Version 1

"The consumption of sweet and savoury, high- and low-fat snack foods, and fruit were measured after both sessions."

_____

_____

## Version 2

A study by Emma J. Boylanda, et al. finds that food advert[isement] exposure has been shown to influence calorie intake and food choice in nine- to eleven-year-olds (263).

_____

_____

## Version 3

A study by Emma J. Boylanda, et al. finds that food advert[isement] exposure has influenced caloric intake and food choice in nine- to eleven-year-olds. They conducted a study with ninety-three kids, younger than seven, about one-third were over-weight (264).

## Version 4

"Their consumption of sweet and savoury, high- and low-fat snack foods, and fruit were measured following both sessions. . . . Beyond their effects on brand choice, exposure to food advertisements (commercials) promotes overconsumption in younger children" (Boylanda et al. 265).

## Version 5

"A study by Emma J. Boylanda, et al. finds that "food advert[isement] exposure has been shown to influence caloric intake and food choice in 9–11 year olds. However, little is known about the effect of food advertisements on feeding behaviour in younger children. Therefore, [they] conducted a study with 93 children aged 5–7 years, 28 of whom were over-weight or obese" (264).

## Version 6

According to research by Emma J. Boylanda, et al., young children (ages five to seven) are influenced by media messages about food. After contact with ten examples of television commercials featuring food, the children's total consumption of food was greater to even a point of overeating (265).

## Version 7

As a result of their study on brand effects on children's consumption of food, Emma J. Boylanda, et al. have come to the conclusion that "exposure to food advertisements (commercials) promotes over-consumption in younger children" (265).

## WRITING A REBUTTAL OR "REFUTATIO"

### Essentials

Select your primary audience, and determine their level of opposition to your position.

Gauge level of resistance to your argument; mark on continuum:

Strongly Disagree   Disagree   Moderate   Agree   Strongly Agree

Determine strategies to persuade audience about your position on topic. Strategies include

appeals to ethos, pathos, and logos; diction, emphasis or deemphasis, and creative repetition.

*What is an effective model for writing a rebuttal? Form*: 3 Es

- Establish (Opposing view to your position)
- Explain (Evidence and Explanation: What? Why?)
- Exploit ("Poke holes" in opposing argument: irrelevant facts or details, logical fallacy, limited or selective viewpoint, thesis applicable only in some cases, and/or points exaggerated)

*What is appropriate diction to use in rebuttals?*
X = your argument; Y = counterargument

- Y argues that . . . ; however, a strong case against Y involves . . .
- X argument holds more weight due to . . .
- While there is truth to Y . . .; X demonstrates . . .
- Y supports_____; however, _____ leads to the conclusion that . . .
  - Ex. Families of murder victims may support the death penalty, but religious arguments against this controversial act lead to the conclusion that even the worst sinners are redeemable and deserve to live.

*Exercise 6*

### Rebuttal or "Refutatio"

Directions: (1) Read "There is Nothing Remarkable About Steroids in Baseball" in *Hardball Times*, originally printed 25 May 2010 and updated 2 March 2018. This opposing viewpoint refutes Fay Vincent's in the article: "Doping Has No Place in Sports" from *The Wall Street Journal*, 24 May 2010, and (2) Label "3 Es" in the Rebuttal ("Refutatio").

"In today's *Wall Street Journal*, former commissioner Fay Vincent offers an editorial (behind a pay wall) on sports' performance-enhancing drug problem. Vincent, reacting to the growing apathy of the public toward confessions of drug use, comments:

> All sports must be played according to the rules in fair competition. We use umpires and referees and other officials to enforce the rules because we know proper adherence to them permits us to determine a winner. If we fail to protect our games by insisting the rules must be obeyed, we will see our favorite sports begin to look like professional wrestling. We will have entertainment and not sports. By dismissing the cheating that seems to permeate all sports these days, we are inviting the gradual demise of the very games we love most.

Vincent goes on to relate concerns about teams aligning with medical research institutions to sponsor doping, leveraging such relationships to develop and produce proprietary means of improving performance through science. Concerned with the erosion of true competition spurred, in part, by the media's apparent decline in outrage, Vincent believes doping in sports is reaching something near critical mass. At such a point, cheating becomes the norm and a return to fairness will be all but impossible.

Vincent argues,

> In a world that has been so enormously enhanced by technology and chemistry—I belong to the generation kept alive by miracle drugs—it is remarkable to see our sports now in a battle to prevent such chemists from ruining the games that give us so much pleasure. The chemists will be hard to beat and this new game has no rules. But to deny that the game is on is absurdly silly and wildly dangerous.

"Remarkable?" Really? It is remarkable that sports are changing along with society? Combating cheating is an important and worthy task for the sports world to undertake, and that can certainly include the media. But to fight societal progress from creeping into sports is a losing battle, and any energy spent trying to freeze sports in time is energy wasted. The single most damaging mistake baseball and its opinion-shapers have made in the entire PED saga has been the direction of focus: backwards. Instead of asking "how do we do this better going forward?," the relevant parties have consistently and wrongheadedly judged future actions by the rules, norms, and events of the past.

Competition *will* be fair, or at least close, because the financial well-being (and thus existence) of the games depends on it. But balance will not be achieved by building walls around sports, freezing them in an era before chemists really began to figure out how to make our bodies work better. The easiest way to aggravate this problem is to deny the natural tendency for sports to evolve with society. I don't know the answer for how to integrate certain types of performance-enhancing drugs fairly into sports. But that's where we're going, and the sports powers that be will serve their games the best by paving the road, not trying to change its direction.

*Exercise 7*

Label three parts of a rebuttal in the counterargument of Angela's research paper, Appendix I

## DETECTING BIAS IN SOURCES

### Essentials

*What is bias?* A point of view that suggests a favorable or unfavorable opinion toward a subject. Biases are strongly held beliefs typically rooted in emotions.

*What is a brief example of bias?* A sixteen-year-old boy looks through the garbage behind a restaurant for awhile. We conclude that he is hungry, but he may have left his keys on the table among napkins, and a server threw them away accidentally.

*How is bias expressed in writing?* Each writer makes choices of which words and ideas to include or exclude, and which points to emphasize or deemphasize. Since writers make decisions about their writing, all text (written, spoken, and visual) includes some level of bias due to the writer's decisions. Think about the key question while reading a published source is this:

Mild                    Moderate                    Strong                    Severe

**Figure 8.1   Level of Biases.**

**Table 8.6   Presence of Biases in Rhetorical Situations**

Presence of Bias in Rhetorical Situations (Contexts)

| Bias | Mild | Moderate | Strong | Severe |
|---|---|---|---|---|
| *Purpose* | To inform | To describe; to explain; to compare/contrast | To persuade | To manipulate |
| *Style: Diction and Tone* | Objective words; detached approach | Objective and thought-provoking words; invested approach | Emotional and/or logical words; highly invested approach | Emotional words; extremely invested approach |
| *Examples* | Driver's Education Manual | Analysis of a newspaper article | Political campaigns | Gangs |
| | Directions to a restaurant | Comparison/contrast of cell-phone options | Fund-raising event for cancer research | Ku Klux Klan |
| | | | | Neo-Nazis |
| | | | | PETA |

What is the extent of bias in this text? (Rather than: Does this published source have a bias or not?)

*What are the ways bias "shows up" in writing?* Descriptive and numerical.

Qualitative (Descriptive)

• Arrangement of words and ideas: What is first, second, third . . . last?
• Diction: positive? negative? mixed?
• Points emphasized or deemphasized, even ignored or absent
• Tone: positive? negative? both? somewhere in-between?

Quantitative (Numerical)

• # of times word or shorter phrase appears
• # of times point is repeated or emphasized (ex. a longer phrase or sentence)
• number and statistics—how are they presented? positive? negative? mixed: positive and negative?

*What are the different degrees or levels of bias?* Depending on writers' purposes, their biases fall on this continuum:

*How do you decide which level of bias to favor in a source for your paper?* This depends on your rhetorical situation, but generally moderately to strong. For instance, if you support more funding for juvenile diabetes, choose articles with a strong bias in agreement with your position. This is true for rebuttals or "Refutatios" too. The recommended range of "Moderate to Strong" is appropriate for most academic, research-based papers.

*Why is bias in writing necessary to assess?* There are two ways to answer this question:

(1) as a researcher, you can wisely select sources that are not extreme in viewpoint, which are commonly based on emotion and opinions rather than logic and facts; and (2) as a writer, you'll gain more respect and credibility if you "come across" as fair-minded and well-informed of your topic and, if writing a research paper, acknowledging a counter argument too. Rather than express extreme opinions (e.g., the government should provide loans to all college students) that always produce exceptions and are generally unrealistic, try to present a moderate-to-strong point of view to achieve your purpose for primary audience.

*Exercise 8*
Return to Exercise 7, identify parts of the rhetorical triangle (e.g., primary audience and purpose); next, do a "bias check" to determine level of bias; finally, decide if you would use this source in an academic paper.

# Chapter 9

# Grammar, Punctuation, and Usage

## ESSENTIALS

*What is the role of the writer regarding grammar and punctuation?* To manage how your readers read your writing, use commas to slow or increase the pace and to build anticipation. As a writer, ask yourself: How does this sentence, paragraph, or essay read? How can I manage the text for the reader to best understand the message?

To decide why there are comma errors in your (or others') writing, examine patterns across essays. See if you need to learn or relearn comma rules, or see if the pattern of errors is due to carelessness, in which case, a review can make you aware of the errors. Eliminate these pesky slips that distract readers from your purpose and message (thesis). Prioritize comma errors and conquer this common problem!

*Where do commas come from?* Used since Ancient Greece, the comma comes from the Greek word: "koptein," which means "to cut off." Therefore, a comma is a "piece cut off." The modern comma was created in the 1400s by Aldus Manutius, an Italian printer, who added a lower curve to a backslash, denoting a pause in speech. After the period, the comma is the most common punctuation mark in English. The default answer to the question of when commas should be used is: "when a reader needs to pause to collect his/her thoughts." Commas are visual substitutes for speakers' oral cues.

*What are the debates about commas?* Debates about comma usage have occurred for many centuries. Does the writer place a "serial" or "Oxford" comma before the coordinating conjunction in a series? Does the writer place a comma after a short introductory phrase? Does a writer decide which information qualifies as essential or nonessential? There are no definitive answers to these questions that fit every genre (newspaper articles, fiction, essays, or academic publications). While there are standard rules relating to comma usage (addressed below) that are used in most writing, comma usage—similar to language—is often situational.

***Example 1***

## COMMA RULES

Place comma(s)...

1. *After an introductory clause or phrase (word groups not containing subject of sentence)*
   Example: After construction of the Statue of Liberty began in June 1885, workers completed the historical sculpture in four months.
   *Introductory clauses or phrases often begin with a preposition:*

> aboard, about, above, across, after, against, along, alongside, amidst, among, around, as, aside, at, atop, before, behind, below, beneath, beside, besides, between, beyond, but, by, during, except, following, for, from, in, inside, into, like, near, next, of, off, on, onto, out, outside, over, plus, regarding, round, save, since, than, through, throughout, to, toward, under, underneath, unlike, until, up, upon, via, with, within, without

Example: From 1984–1986, the government replaced the torch and other structures.

2. *Around nonessential or nonrestrictive information; do not place commas around essential or restrictive information*
   *Adjectival Clauses:*
   *"that" begins essential clauses*
   Example: The statue that was constructed in France was built as a sign of comradery.
   *"which" begins nonessential clauses*
   Example: The Statue of Liberty, which is a light shade of green, has stood on New York Harbor for over 100 years.
   *Appositives*
   *Nonessential = commas*
   Example: The Statue of Liberty, a large metal woman, was created by Frederic-Auguste Bartholdi.
   *Essential = no commas*
   Example: French sculptor Gustave Eiffel built a copper model of the Statue of Liberty.
3. *After an attributive tag, before a quotation*
   Example: Emma Lazarus' declaration, "Give me your tired, your poor, your huddled masses yearning to breathe
   free" helped to raise money for the Statue of Liberty.
4. *Before adverb clause in middle of a sentence*
   Example: Immigrants coming from overseas often identified with the Statue of Liberty, because it represented the freedom and grandeur that was America.
5. *In a series*
   Example: The Statue of Liberty is grand, stunning, and elegant.
6. *Between coordinating adjectives not joined by "and"*
   Example: The generous, kind French first coordinated with the United States to honor their lasting friendship by creating the Statue of Liberty.
7. *Before coordinating conjunctions between independent clauses* (FANBOYS)

| Independent Clause | , for | Independent Clause |
| | , and | |
| | , nor | |
| | , but | |
| | , or | |
| | , yet | |
| | , so | |

Examples:
   We visit Ellis Island every year, and we enjoy looking in the archives to find information about our genealogy.
   Ellis Island—part of the Statue/ of Liberty National monument—opened for tours in 1976, yet this historical place was dedicated eleven years earlier by President Johnson.
8. *After subordinating clauses that begin sentences:*

**Table 9.1   Subordinating Conjunctions**

| After | Although | As |
|---|---|---|
| Besides | Before | Below |
| Even though | In order to | Nevertheless |
| Since | So that | Though |
| When | Whenever | Wherever |

Even though we visited New York City last summer, we are visiting city again to see a new Broadway shows.
   After each show, we ate at a famous Italian restaurant near Times Square.

## COMMON COMMA PROBLEMS

*Comma Splice*: Two independent clauses or sentences mistakenly separated (or joined) by a comma.
   Ellis Island and the Statue of Liberty are important stops on a visit to New York City, people take the ferry to visit both historical sites.
   *Run-On Sentence*: Two independent clauses or sentences not separated by a comma or other punctuation.
   The Ellis Island Visitors Museum hosts millions of visitors each year visitors can walk where immigrants were detained before they began their new lives in America.

### Exercise 1

### Commas

Directions: Add commas where necessary in the sentences. There may be sentences that do not require commas.

1. When we watched the film everyone was silent and riveted.
2. We telephoned the diplomatic center and we reached a representative promptly.
3. We telephoned the diplomatic center and reached a representative promptly.

4. For example people are living on the streets because they cannot make ends meet.
5. On the street corner there was always a man who would beg me for money and he would talk about religion.
6. I joined the military specifically the Coast Guard because I can make an impact on the world.
7. Mary Shelley's novel *Frankenstein* or the *Modern Prometheus* was first published in 1818.
8. We participated in the summer program; therefore we may have a higher chance of acceptance at the liberal arts college.
9. Though the football game was terribly exciting the outcome was overshadowed by the brawl among temperamental players.
10. We watched the game on our new HD television and ate a lot of junk food.
11. We wanted the Midwestern team to win because we are long-time residents of Illinois.
12. We look forward to the Super bowl and we plan to host a game party that day.
13. In Homer's epic narrative the hero Odysseus faces many dangers such as the god Poseidon the Sirens and the goddess Calypso.
14. The base of the Statue of Liberty is granite but the igneous rock is from Stony Creek Connecticut.
15. When we prepared for backpacking trip across Europe we packed extra socks soap and phone chargers.

## ADVERB CLAUSES AND COMMA USAGE

• Adverb clauses answer the questions: How? When? Where? To What Extent?
• Adverb clauses contain: subordinating conjunctions, subjects, and verbs.

Subordinating conjunctions include: when, if, because, although, since, while, before, after, unless

• When the adverb clause appears at the beginning of the sentence, add a comma:
    Ex. When I arrive at the dormitory, I will meet my new roommate. (#1)

• When the adverb clause appears at the end of the sentence, do not add a comma.
    Ex. I will meet my new roommate when I arrive at the dormitory. (#2)

Directions: Referring to the comma rules above, add commas (where necessary), and label each sentence with #1 if clause is in first part of the sentence or with #2 if clause is in second part of the sentence.

### *Exercise 2*

1. I usually have coffee after I wake up in the morning._____
2. If I have homework I'll finish it after dinner in Rockman Library._____
3. When I finish my homework I usually read a Science Fiction book for pleasure._____
4. I often listen to music only on my iPhone though I have many CDs._____
5. I read in bed because reading helps me fall asleep._____
6. Before I take an exam I re-read my notes and do practice formulas._____
7. While I finished my laundry, I completed my lab report and studied for my Psychology exam._____
8. Since we have a fall break we are traveling to Vermont to see the foliage._____
9. I hurry to Chemistry II class in Taylor Hall because the transitions between classes are only 10 minutes._____
10. Unless there is a lot of snow and sleet on the roads the school will open tomorrow._____

### End Punctuation with Quotations

*Place punctuation marks (periods, commas, semicolons) inside quotation marks when there is no citation.*

Annie Proulx wrote a poem: "Inspiration? Head Down the Back Road, and Stop for the Yard Sales."

*Place punctuation marks (periods, commas, semicolons) outside citations in sentence with quotation marks.*

Proulx wants readers to "fold down page corners and scribble in margins of books they find at yard sales" (1).

*Semicolons*

Use a semicolon to join two independent clauses

Sam Foster, a plastics developer, sold the first pair of sunglasses in America; they were mass-produced starting in 1929.

*Use a semicolon before conjunctive adverbs and transitional phrases*

**Examples of Conjunctive Adverbs and Transitional Phrases:**
as a result in addition on the contrary consequently in fact similarly for example meanwhile therefore however nevertheless thus

## CONJUNCTIVE ADVERBS AND TRANSITIONAL PHRASES

| | ; as a result, ;<br>   consequently, | |
|---|---|---|
| Independent<br>Clause | ; however,<br>; nevertheless,<br>; therefore, | Independent<br>Clause |

*Use a semicolon before conjunctive adverbs between independent clauses.*

In twelfth-century China, judges wore dark glasses in court; as a result, they were able to conceal their emotions from the jury of twelve free men.

*Use a semicolon to separate items in a series or to separate clauses when they contain commas.*

The inventors of sunglasses included James Ayscough, who created tinted-lens spectacles in 1752; Sam Foster, who industrialized mass-produced Foster Grants; and Edwin H. Land, who established polarized sunglasses in 1936.

### *Exercise 3*

### Commas and Semicolons for Compound Sentences

Rules for commas and semicolons for compound sentences:

a.  Joined by comma and coordinating conjunction:
    fanboys: for, and, nor, boy, or, yet, so

Ex. We are flying to Colorado for the holidays, and we plan to ski in Aspen.

b.  Joined with semicolon
    Ex. We are flying to Colorado for the holidays; we plan to ski in Aspen.

c.  Joined with semicolon, subordinating conjunction, comma
    Subordinating Conjunctions: as a result, consequently, for example, however, in fact, nevertheless, therefore
    Ex. We are flying to Colorado for the holidays; however, we can stay only a few days.

Directions: For each compound sentence, punctuate using one of the above choices (a, b, or c)

1.  The ski club members have skied in New Hampshire_____they enjoyed the beautiful scenery of the White Mountains.
2.  Snowboarding in Vermont is a fun way to spend winter break_____ our budget allows us to stay for the whole week.
3.  We found some inexpensive lodging and skiing packages_____ the Stowe Lodge offers the best deal for students.
4.  In addition to skiing, we hiked the trails around Aspen_____ we ate at a few smokehouse restaurants.
5.  Skiers and snowboarders are particular about conditions_____ they prefer either ice or powdery snow_____ but not both.

## CAPITALIZATION

### Essentials

*When do writers use (or not use) capitalization for words and phrases?* Capitalize proper or specific nouns; don't capitalize common or general nouns.

*What are the more typical words and phrases that cause confusion about using capitalization?* See below:

These categories generally require capital letters because they are proper (specific) nouns:

• *Academic subjects and courses*: English 102, Advanced Placement Biology, Psychology 203
• *Areas and regions* (caps): Northeast, the South, Pacific Northwest, the Eastern Seaboard

- *Historical events, movements, periods, and documents*: Battle of Gettysburg, Occupy Wall Street, Bill of Rights
- *Languages*: French, German, Hindi, English, Haitian Creole
- *Religions*: Buddhism, Christianity, Judaism
- *Seasons*: Fall Semester, Summer Rhythm-and-Blues Festival

These words and phrases do not require capital letters because they are common (general) nouns:

- *Academic subjects and courses*: history, psychology, math, business, sociology
- *Areas:* north of shoreline, eastern sun, western mountains, southern direction
- *History*: uprising, protest, war, election
- *Religious references:* church, synagogue, temple, mosque
- *Seasons:* winter, spring, summer, fall

*Refer to an online grammar/punctuation/ usage program for additional explanations of capitalization.

## *Exercise 4*

### Capitalization

Directions: Capitalize all relevant titles, names, locations, and other proper nouns.

1. After leaving his house, Jeremy headed northwest toward the movie theater to see harry potter and the sorcerer stone.
2. Since I ran out of ink for the printer, I had to drive on a freezing winter day to buy cartridges.
3. Though it was a very cold winter day, juanita went for a run and felt invigorated.
4. Although there have been extraordinary figures in world literature, people consider homer and shakespeare two of the greatest authors to have ever graced this earth.
5. People often think that the battle of gettysburg was the bloodiest in the civil war; however, the battle of antietam claims this fact.
6. Even though it is widely considered the toughest course, I wanted to take professor adam's english and professor torok's multivariable calculus courses.
7. When I took a religion class, we studied the bible, the koran, and the torah in-depth to compare the virtues of each holy work.
8. Problems in the middle east escalated today due to a bombing of a local oil pipeline.
9. Senator Howard's campaign is in full force thanks to her team who work in the Rayburn building on independence ave in the southwest area of washington d.c.
10. My nephew, C.J., is a sophomore at purdue university in west lafayette, indiana.
11. The u.s. coast guard conducted a successful operation for which its florida crew received praise from the national transportation safety board.
12. The *scarlet letter, the great gatsby, the color purple,* and *her eyes were watching god* are several of the most common novels in American high-school English curriculums.
13. We could not decide if we wanted to buy a macpro or dell computer to play batman: arkham knight and destiny video games.
14. After the gilded age of the 1920s, the great depression of the 1930s was a fall after rise of artistic culture.
15. This summer, we plan to visit yellowstone national park and jackson hole, wyoming.

## *Punctuating Titles: Quotation Marks, Italics, and/or Underlining*

Shorter works—those "inside" of longer pieces of literature—are quoted.

Longer works—those "outside" of shorter pieces of literature—are italicized or underlined. (They are interchangeable.) Depending on style, publication, assignment, or editorial guidelines, italicize or underline longer titles. The rule-of-thumb is consistency, regardless of whether you are italicizing or underlining titles.

Exceptions: Religious works are not underlined nor italicized. For example, The Bible, The Torah, the Koran, and The Book of Mormon.

Titles of student papers are not italicized, underlined, or quoted. For example, Explorations in the Deep Sea

**Table 9.2   Punctuating Titles of Shorter and Longer Works of Literature**

| *Shorter Works of Literature* | *Longer Works of Literature* |
|---|---|
| Essay<br>"The Fiction of Langston Hughes" | Collection of Essays<br>*A Collection of Essays* by George Orwell |
| Act or Scene<br>Act 2; scene 1: "A Room in Polonius' House" | Play or Drama<br>*Hamlet* by Shakespeare or<br>*Fences* by August Wilson |
| Article, Blog, Column<br>"Can Coupons Help Curb Obesity?"<br>"3 Healthy Breakfast Ideas that Reduce Afternoon Cravings"<br>"Google tries to rethink email with 'inbox'" & "D.C. Sports Blog" | Journal, Magazine, Newspaper<br>*Journal of the American Medical Association*<br>*Fitness*<br>*Washington Post* |
| Chapter, Section, (ex. Preface & Epilogue), Vignette | Reference Books: Dictionary or Encyclopedia<br>*Oxford English Dictionary, World Book Encyclopedia, Roget's*<br>     *Thesaurus* |
| "The Truth of the Green Light"<br>"Chapter 1"<br>"The Chimes of Big Ben" | Novel, Novella<br>*Invisible Man*<br>*The Great Gatsby, Of Mice and Men* |
| Clip, Scene<br>"Age of Heroes" | Film or DVD<br>*The Lord of the Rings: The Return of the King* |
| Commercial, Episode<br>"Geico: Meditation with Maxwell the Pig"<br> "The Parking Garage"<br>"A Streetcar Named Marge" | Television Show<br>*Seinfeld*<br>*The Simpsons* |
| Page<br>"Protecting Your Family from Cybercrime" | Pamphlet<br>*Terrorism: What the Public Needs to Know* |
| Episode, Scene<br>"The Land of Sweets" &<br>"Destruction of Don Quixote's Library" | Performance<br>*The Nutcracker* ballet & *Don Quixote* opera |
| Short Poem<br>"Death be not proud" by John Donne<br>"Hope" by Emily Dickinson | Long Poem (ex. Epic Poem)<br>*The Iliad, The Aeneid, The Rime of the Ancient Mariner* |
| Short Story<br>"Sonny's Blues" by James Baldwin | Anthology or Collection of Literature<br>*Twenty Great American Short Stories* |
| Song<br>"A Sky Full of Stars" by Coldplay | CD or Album<br>*Keeps Gettin' Better: A Decade of Hits* by Christina Aguilera |
| Web page<br>"Apple issues security warning for iCloud" | Website<br>*Apple.com* |

## *Exercise 5*

### Punctuating Titles

***Directions: Punctuate each title with quotations, italics, or underlining.***

1. I searched Netflix and found a British series, Broadchurch, which is a crime drama about a young boy murdered in a small town, and everyone is a suspect.
2. In high school English class, we read The Great Gatsby by F. Scott Fitzgerald and Beloved by Toni Morrison.
3. In college English class, we read Maya Angelou's poem Phenomenal Woman, and Homer's epic poem, *The Odyssey.*
4. Have you read the article, French Police Destroys Virus that Hit Nearly 1 Million Computers, in Time magazine?
5. We joined the millions of people who subscribe to Amazon Prime to watch old films such as The Godfather series and Apocalypse Now.
6. My favorite episode of The Lord of the Rings is The Return of the King.
7. Bruno Mars won a Grammy award for his album, 24K Magic, which includes songs: 24K Magic, Perm, and Finesse.
8. Paula found an article, Biochemical Breakthroughs in the 21$^{st}$ Century, in the database, EBSCO.
9. We watched the Geico commercial entitled: More insurance for less money.
10. Most college freshmen have read Faulkner's short story, A Rose for Emily.

# Chapter 10

# Visual Arguments

## ESSENTIALS

*How are visual arguments defined?* As images that speak for themselves and send a message to an audience, images are everywhere. In any given day, images on the Internet, television, e-books, and hard-copy (print) occupy our lives. In these media, there are advertisements, billboards, commercials, graphics, films, paintings, photos, videos, tables, charts, posters, flyers, cartoons, and others. We "read" images in ways that are similar to as well as different from the ways we read written words.

*What are our common responses to images?* Though we decide quickly if we like or dislike an image, our responses, especially when we evaluate images, go beyond our initial favorable or unfavorable responses. Often, we respond emotionally, logically, and/or ethically to visual texts.

*What are the fundamental rhetorical principles of analyzing a visual argument?* (1) Situation, (2) Strategies, and (3) Format

## RHETORICAL SITUATION OF THE ADVERTISEMENT

Creator(s): *Who* created the visual images? Individual, group, organization, business

- Topic: *What* is the subject?
- Thesis: *What* is the central message?
- Audience: *Who* is the primary audience? *Who* else is affected by or invested in the image?
- Context: *When* and *Where* does the image appear?
- Purpose: *Why* is the image visible?

In summary, who created the image? For whom? When? Where? Why?

## RHETORICAL STRATEGIES OF THE ADVERTISEMENT

a. Exigency: "A problem, lack, or need" (informally) and "an imperfection marked by urgency; a defect, obstacle, something waiting to be done" (Bitzer 8).

　What is the urgency of the advertisement? What is the answer to: So what?

b. Rhetorical Appeals:
- Logos = appeal to logic
- Pathos = appeal to emotions
- Ethos = appeal to ethics

Features of Advertisement:

- Tone: casual, informal, or playful impression
- Diction
- Point of View

## RHETORICAL FORMAT OF THE ADVERTISEMENT

- Color
- Images and graphics
- Space and layout
- Type
- Variations in type (size, boldface, italics, or caps) can direct the readers' attention to an argument's structure and highlight main points
- Two or three font styles per document
- Consistent patterns of type
- Overall readability, visual appeal, and suitability

　Note: All four design components can reinforce and support one another to achieve a rhetorical effect.

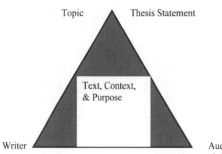

**Figure 10.1   Full Rhetorical Situation.**

**Figure 10.2   Chipotle Advertisement: "Eat for a Change."** Copyright @ Chipotle.

*Examples 10.2–10.5*

*Exercise 1: Examining Advertisements 10.1 & 10.2*

Drawing from Pts. I–III above, analyze these aspects of each advertisement by answering these questions:

1. What is the rhetorical situation surrounding the ad?
2. What are strategies used in the ad?
3. What is the format of the ad?

4. Draw a conclusion about the effectiveness of the ad. Does it fulfill its purpose for its primary audience?

Exercise 2

Browse the Internet (e.g., newspaper, magazine, and company) and locate an image that lends itself well to visual analysis. Answer the questions in Pts. I, II, and IV above. Draw a conclusion at the end and compare advertisements from the same company or institution or from different companies that sell the same product.

**Figure 10.3    Chipotle Advertisement: "Tastes Delicious."** Copyright @ Chipotle.

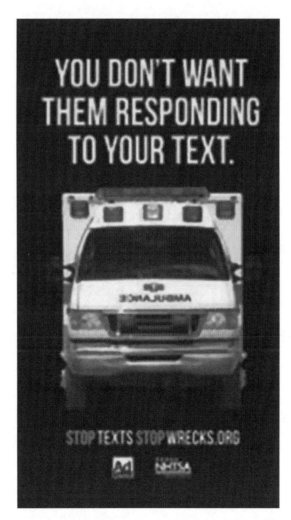

**Figure 10.4    www.stoptextsstopwrecks.com. Advertisement: "You Don't Want Them Responding to Your Text."** Copyright @ stoptextsstopwrecks.

**Figure 10.5    Public Service Announcement: "Wildfire embers."** https://www.psacentral.org/home.do.

Visual Arguments

# Appendix I

## *Sample Research Paper with Audience Analysis*

### *Angela, College Freshman, Composition Course*

### *Audience Analysis for Angela's Research Paper*

The primary audience for my research paper is parents and educators who influence male students. They are a diversified audience, range in age from thirty to fifty years, and racial and middle socioeconomic class. Presumably, the main age restriction would be on the boys in middle school or high school, approximately thirteen to eighteen years of age. My educated, professional audience holds several viewpoints on single-sex education; however, I have written my argument assuming the audience is either neutral or opposed to single-sex education, more likely the former. I would expect the boys in my audience to lean toward the opposed side, based on my experience discussing single-sex education with my peers. My secondary audience in this paper is my instructor and classmates. I anticipate that these people would be, in general, unfamiliar with my topic unless they attended single-sex schools. If asked to choose they would not be in favor of single-sex education, for the reasons stated above. Overall, I am seeking to convince parents and educators to take a closer look at boys' learning (or lack thereof) in single-sex schools.

(Student's Research Paper. Reprinted with permission of student writer.)

## ANGELA'S RESEARCH PAPER: REFLECTING CLASSICAL MODEL: ARISTOTLE'S SIX PARTS OF AN ARGUMENT

### [Exordium: Introduction]

The bell rings. Time to get the academic day started. Students file in, one after another, taking their places and pulling out their books, eager to begin learning. Class commences, and the students listen attentively to their teacher, drinking in the lecture and conversing on the book's content. However, something appears a little different about this particular class. The rows are filled with one kind of student. This institute is an all-boys' school, and, as such, prepares these young men in a manner unmatched by other schools.

Much research has been done into the effects of single-sex schooling on women, with many positive results. The benefits of such an education are rarely acknowledged in regards to another demographic, though—boys. [Partition/Thesis Statement—*Partitio*] Single-sex schools offer numerous advantages to boys as they encourage exploration in diverse academic material and promote engagement within the classroom and beyond, while free from the typical social expectations that plague the academic community.

### [Narration/Background—*Narratio*]

As dismal as it may appear, studies provide evidence that boys in today's coeducational schools are struggling. Whitmire, a researcher in the field, has analyzed extensively the performance of young men in academics, and reaped disappointing results in his 2009 published work, *Why Boys Fail*. In situations where a student needs to repeat a grade, or faces suspension or expulsion, the pupil in question is more likely to be male than female (212). Many boys purse college education, though, and tend to show greater mastery of concepts in STEM classes. Historically, there has been a need for parents and educators to examine how to better support boys in technical and nontechnical subjects. Twice as many parents had to discuss their sons' issues with an expert than had to do so with daughters (213). By twelfth grade, more than a quarter of males rate as "below basic" writers on federal tests, compared to "11 percent of females. Just 16 percent of males at that age test as proficient/advanced writers, compared to 31 percent of females. In reading, a third of male students that age fall below basic, compared to 22 percent of females. Only 29 percent of male students are reading at the proficient/advanced levels, compared to 41 percent of females" (214). Clearly, there exist discrepancies between the academic achievements of some male students and female students. Research from single-sex education of boys shows greater gains of academic achievement than from co-ed education. The results show a reversal of a downward trend of low grades for some boys, and a closure of gap between girls' and boys' learning in an important early study (Kelly and Gurian 56).

## [Confirmation/Background— *Confirmatio*]

Addressing these issues in boys' education to provide them with a quality academic environment is an issue of increasing importance. The task proves challenging indeed in a classroom mixed with both boys and girls, as the genders are naturally unique. One need only look to the research done by Dr. Leonard Sax, and his text *Why Gender Matters* to better understand the differences between the male and female brain organization. Consider the differences in brain use when concerned with that touchiest of subjects: spatially oriented activities, such as navigation. According to Sax,

> Neuroscientists have found that young women and young men use different areas in the brain when they navigate: young women use the cerebral cortex while young men use the hippocampus, a nucleus deep inside the brain that is not activated in women's brains during navigational tasks. (Sax 26)

Consequently, women understand directions in terms of "tangible" landmarks and sights; men utilize directions and measurements. The different genders stimulate different regions of brain to understand locations and routes (25). Thus, girls and boys understand spatial and directional concepts differently, thus prompting the need to teach these topics using methods best suited to each gender.

Unique natures persist between teenage boys and girls relative to emotions as well. In a teenage boy, the brain activities dealing with the stress and other unfortunate emotional turmoil of young adulthood take place in the amygdala—the same location as in children as young as seven years old. In contrast, a girl of the same age has already established a link between this less-developed area and the more complex cerebral cortex, which enables her to better express her feelings. In contrast, "Asking a teenage boy to talk about how he feels is a question guaranteed to make most boys uncomfortable," Sax insists. "You're asking him to make connections between two parts of his brain that don't normally communicate" (30). Thus, a girl and a boy heading into adulthood do experience similar feelings. They simply cannot express them to the same level (29).

To add a foundation of concrete evidence to the theoretical side, Sax presents evidence for physical differences. Studies performed on newborns affirm that baby girls react more strongly to sounds of varying ranges than baby boys. Due to this increased sensitivity toward sound, what is to a girl loud shouting might be to a boy perfectly normal (Sax 17). Imagine, then, a teacher in a classroom. As Sax explains, sometimes it is not that a boy deliberately ignores his teachers; rather, he cannot hear them and their lessons (88). Similarly, studies of preteens indicate that boys tolerate sounds better than girls, as it takes ten times the level of volume to distract a boy from a task than a girl. The classroom environment then puts this to the test. Will the noise distract the students, or not? It could boil down to their genders (18). Sax also explains how boys' and girls' eyes respond with significant variance to colors. Ask for artistic creations, and girls will present drawings with beige, red, and a plethora of other colors that appeal to the cells that make up their eyes, known as P cells. Boys, conversely, will use just a few colors, probably black, blue, and other such shades to express themselves; these colors are well-adjusted to the M cells that populate a boy's eyes (24). Interestingly enough, these same cells also affect what the drawings are likely to depict. Boys will draw something "happening," while girls will draw still-life images. P cells look at the objects; M cells look at the motion (22). These various gender differences are diverse and undeniable. Knowing this, the schools today face the challenge of finding a place for boys in the educational system that will cater to their innate learning styles and dissimilarities from girls, and provide them with a rich academic experience.

One of the most logical and visible signs of the benefits of such an education is the teachers' ability to create a curriculum serving the boys' specific intellectual strengths, and the positive response of the boys to their schoolwork. An article in *The Guardian* written by Rachel Williams quotes a researcher studying educational methods, Abigail James, who describes how English, a subject commonly shunned, intrigues boys in single-sex schools. The article insists that seeing young women surpass them in verbal skills leaves young men frustrated (Williams 1). Even Ginger Miller, an associate director of college counseling at the all-boys Landon School in Bethesda, Maryland, agrees that young men struggle more with English. In a personal interview, she described how boys can discover information on a topic, but struggle to absorb it to the depth that girls do, thus turning comprehension into an exasperating competition they cannot win (Interview). At an all-boys' school, this inferiority complex need not exist. Since they teach in a boys-only environment, teachers can use those readings and exercises that appeal to boys. James states as an example, "Boys in boys' schools 'loved' to pen verse because they enjoy the inherent structure in poems'" (James, qtd. in Williams). The same sort of concept applies to boys' overall learning styles. Miller discussed the need of her male students to physically engage in hands-on learning. Teachers cannot expect boys to sit still and quietly listen in the way that girls do (Interview). Thus, in an all-boys classroom, the teacher can create activities to address this physical energy in boys, whether they are races to write answers on the board or doing skits instead of papers. The teacher in an all-boys' classroom can recognize the physical and mental differences in which a boy learns and can adjust accordingly. For example, as is presented by Sax, perhaps he or she must speak at a volume that would drive girls crazy; however, there are no girls to bother. Consequently, the boys need not lose out to the intricacies of gender differences that influence coed classrooms (Sax 18). Single-sex classrooms give a new kind of freedom to teachers: the promise of implementing a curriculum built to reflect the boys' innate learning differences.

In addition to the purely academic tasks, boys in single-sex schools also display strong interest in diversifying their pursuits outside of school and engaging in the classroom activities. In particular, boys educated in single-sex schools are more inclined to seek roles in the arts. As is asserted in Williams' article, "Boys at single sex schools were said to be more likely to get involved in cultural and artistic activities that helped develop their emotional expressiveness, rather than feeling they had to conform to the 'boy code' of hiding their emotions to be a 'real man'" (Williams 1). Miller also explained the more practical reasons boys at single-sex schools become involved in the arts—they take on the roles that girls often fill. She used the example of musicians in the orchestra; the seats must be filled with boys and boys alone (Interview). Thus, boys in single-sex schools have greater opportunity to take part in the arts, and, more importantly, eagerly do so, according to Miller. They are on the way to breaking free from the stereotypes that performance and design are for girls alone, and are immersing themselves in the rich cultural and emotional experiences that come with the arts. Their creative genius is unleashed in yet another way, thanks to the arts encouraged in a single-sex school.

Not only do they focus on newfound interests in enriching extracurriculars, boys in single-sex schools speak out, willingly expressing their opinions in the classroom setting, as well as their imaginations and creative talents. Miller indicated that having only boys in the room contributes to "tangent" conversations, and sidelines stemming from the primary topic that perhaps would not come up with young women in the room. She presented the example of a discussion on hazing in the military, and asserted in an interview that such a blunt discussion could very well be restrained had female students been present. In essence, the all-male classroom is more open, allowing for boys to express themselves more freely without the fear of offending female classmates. In addition, Miller noted that she has observed the tendency of girls to participate more garrulously in such conversations. Once the class removes girls, it is up to the boys to generate discussion—they are not overshadowed by their more talkative female counterparts (Interview). The boys' classroom nurtures discussion and open expression, an experience that can never be quite the same in a coeducational situation. This freedom of expression applies not only to opinions and sharing but also to creation and analytical processes. Sax delivers a detailed recount of an all-boys' classroom studying the novel *Lord of the Flies*. As would be expected, the boys were assigned a project responding to the novel. Sax recalled once writing an essay about being in one of the character's shoes—an exercise in emotions, which, as was discovered earlier, does not hold the same learning potential in boys as it does for girls. Accordingly, Sax was surprised to see that the boys had prepared maps of the island in the book. How would such an assignment benefit the boys? It certainly was against the norm for a book that is usually analyzed from a philosophical and standpoint. But, evidently, the norm was not shown in this novel:

> I noticed that the boys were really involved in the assignment. Williams was building on these boys' natural interests and their strength: spatial relations, mapmaking. He was keeping the assignment objective [. . .]
>
> And the skills these boys were learning are useful: carefully deconstructing a text, finding clues hundreds of pages apart, and using those clues to assemble a coherent picture. That sort of puzzle-solving is a skill that more of us could use. [. . .] Analytical deconstruction of a text is at least as useful as being able to write an imaginative essay about "how you would feel in a given situation. (Sax 110)

Thus, Williams' boys, alone in their class, expressed the mental pictures and thoughts they had in a way specifically suited to their male learning style. This is the success one sees in the single-sex classroom, a window for expression that remains closed in a coed institution.

One of the most evident benefits of all-boys school—albeit perhaps a clichéd one—is reducing age-old gender stereotypes and social expectations from the academic community. When asked about the benefits of single-sex education, Miller cited the absence of the opposite gender as a definite advantage. Boys cannot seek attention from girls when they are not present (Interview). Miller does not stand alone in her beliefs, either. Another interviewee, Danny Spelta, associate director of college counseling at a coed institution in Washington, D.C., named the Edmund Burke School, offered similar thoughts. His observations affirm that a female-free environment provides fewer distractions for boys (Interview). The lowered distraction appears to be a consistent feature of research into benefits of single-sex schools. Social liberation can even be tied back into the William's article—"The absence of girls gives boys the chance to develop without pressure to conform to a stereotype" (Williams 1). Perhaps this is what makes the difference in classes taught by Steve O'Keefe at the Burke School. In an e-mail interview, O'Keefe stated: "Boys in same gender classes [. . .] are less inclined to act out, interrupt, flirt, disrupt or show off. In same gender classes participants seem less afraid to be wrong and are more willing to take intellectual risks" (O'Keefe). Boys among boys do not have to worry about their image in the eyes of women. They can instead be concerned with their studies and developing their own opinions.

Having graduated from a single-sex school, I can attest to the validity of these statements. Though I am female, the general concept of this kind of schooling and the basic benefits still correspond—social and gender roles being a significant similarity. During high school, I walked into class every day with nobody watching me but my female peers. During class, we focused on academic material, and in the hallways, joked around with one other. Teamwork, leadership, discussions, and studying monopolized our class time, not trying to attract the cute boy standing a few lockers away. Appearance merited only a passing thought, not much beyond the chance to display our favorite mismatched jewelry and scarves. Upon graduation, I enrolled at the U.S. Coast Guard Academy, which is a male-dominated institution. Once school started, I began to notice myself changing. I suddenly cared surprisingly more about how I looked during the day, and became much more focused on my own femininity. My behavior began to shift to a "girlier" way of acting, the more stereotypical. At first, I attributed this to the joys of being out of "boot camp" and being allowed to express myself as an individual. However, reflecting upon the change, I believe it was influenced significantly by the presence of young men at the Academy, and my focus on building relationships with them and establishing my identity as a woman. Romance and feminism dominated my thoughts, not academics. I had fallen into the trap of distraction by the opposite sex—something I never experienced in my single-sex school. I am female, not male. Regardless, my experience attests to the influence of the opposite gender on one's educational experience, and reinforces Williams' ideas—removal of the opposite sex does make a difference in a classroom.

## [Rebuttal-Refutatio]

Even in light of these many positive aspects of single-sex education, there persist many threadbare arguments against such a system. However, upon inspection, these arguments prove invalid. Silva participates in a Washington, D.C. Think Tank that studies issues in education. Her article published through the Opposing Viewpoints database provides arguments against the establishment of single-sex schools. Frequently, Silva insists that single-sex education, in general, produces no noticeable benefits (1). This becomes hard to believe when one uncovers the information presented already regarding the differences in boys in single-sex schools relative to studies in the arts and English, the overall more open environment, and the liberation from social expectations and standards. Silva even weakens her own argument by citing a source that blatantly acknowledges the existence of single-sex schooling benefits. "One study by researcher Riordan found that poor and minority students performed better academically in single-sex schools. However, Riordan acknowledges these students likely did better because single-sex schools have a greater academic orientation and focused curriculum" (2). Accidentally, Silva reaffirms one of the main criteria of single-sex schools in the midst of her complaints—single-sex schools allow for tailored curriculums that indeed give an advantage to their students. Silva also insists that there are few differences between the ways that girls and boys learn, but does not delve deeply into that argument (2). Her vague protestations stand feebly in front of Sax, who, beyond having a medical degree of his own, has evidently researched the topic heavily; multiple sources consulted during the research of this report cited his work. Silva focused also on the practical impacts of single-sex education—the cost of building new schools, the idea that discrimination lawsuits could follow, the need to get teachers, and so on (3). If one were to use these arguments, then new schools should never be erected, regardless of the genders they serve. There are high costs to make new facilities and expand educational horizons. Shall we revert back to the one-room schoolhouses of early America? Conclusively, Silva's arguments are unable to stand against the logic of single-sex schools.

A struggle exists in today's educational system. A struggle manifests in a young boy, different from his female counterparts. He is forced to be a piece in a puzzle that never fits quite right. He grows frustrated, he falls behind, he and his gifts are lost to an educational system that just does not work for him. This struggle necessitates a new environment—an environment of those who think like him, learn like him, and explore like him. Denial of the differences has no place in today's contemporary school systems, and must be addressed. Single-sex schools do so. Their surroundings are open to emotional and creative release. Their classrooms are free from distractions and unfair societal expectations. Their curriculum is carefully crafted to give boys lessons they can truly learn. Today's schools hold responsibility for teaching and empowering young boys, turning them into young men of wisdom and knowledge. Single-sex schools form the hands with which the world grips on to the future of boys.

## WORKS CITED

"Interview with Ginger Miller." Telephone Interview. 15 and 18 November 2013.

"Interview with Danny Spelta." Telephone Interview. 19 November 2013.

"Interview with Steve O'Keefe." Email Interview. 20 November 2013.

King, Kelley and Michael Gurian. "Teaching to the Minds of Boys." *Educational Leadership*. 64,2 (2006): 56–58, 60–61. Print.

Sax, Leonard. *Why Gender Matters: What Parents and Teachers Need to Know About the Emerging Science of Sex Differences*. New York: Doubleday, 2005. Print.

Silva, Elena. "Single-Sex Schools Will Not Improve Education." *Education*. Ed. David Haugen and Susan Musser. Detroit: Greenhaven Press, 2009. *Opposing Viewpoints*. Rpt. from "Boys and Girls Are More Alike in School Than They Are Different." DelawareOnline.com. 2008. *Opposing Viewpoints in Context*. Web. 11 November 2013.

*Why Boys Fail: Saving Our Sons from an Educational System That's Leaving Them Behind*. New York: AMACOM, 2010. Print.

Williams, Rachel. "Single-Sex Schools Help Boys to Enjoy Arts, Says Study." *The Guardian*. Guardian News and Media Limited, 19 January 2010. Web. November 2013.

## WORKS CONSULTED

*American Friends of Tel Aviv University*. "Keep Boys and Girls Together, TAU Research Suggests." American Friends Tel Aviv University: Expanding the Future. American Friends of Tel Aviv University, 11 April 2008. Web. November 2013.

Anonymous. "DC Area Secular Single Gender High School for Boys?" DC Urban Moms and Dads. D.C. Urban Moms and Dads, 15 February 2012. Web. November 2013.

CBS. "Intellectual Gender Gap?" *Sunday Morning*. CBS
    Interactive Inc., 11 February 2009. Web. November
    2013.

Edmund Burke School. School Profile 2013–2014. Wash-
    ington, D.C.: 2013–2014. Electronic.

Landon School. Profile 2013–2014. Bethesda, MD: 2013–
    2014. Print.

National Association for Single-Sex Public Educa-
    tion. "Single-Sex vs. Coed: The Evidence. NASSPE:
    National Association for Single-Sex Public Education."
    MCRDAB D/b/a/ NASSPE, 2006-2013. Web. Novem-
    ber 2013.

*Washingtonian Magazine*. "Coed Private Schools in
    DC, Maryland, & Virginia." 1 November 2006. Web.
    November 2013.

# Appendix II

## *Answer Keys to Major Exercises*

### *Other Exercises Have Answers That May Vary*

**EXERCISE 1: (CHAPTER 4)**

In the following quotations, do the speakers make an appeal strongly based on ethos, pathos, or logos? Several quotes reflect primary and secondary appeals.

a) _____ "If we started in 1960, and we said that as productivity goes up, then the minimum wage is going to go up the same. If that were the case, the minimum wage today would be about $22 an hour. . . . So my question is, what happened to the other $14.75?" (Elizabeth Warren) *Logos*

b) _____ "I have reasoned this out of my mind, there was one of two things I had a right to, liberty or death; if I could not have one, I'd have the other" (Harriet Tubman) *Ethos, Pathos*

c) _____"I have decided to stick with love. Hate is too great a burden to bear." (MLK, Jr.) *Pathos*

d) _____"[T]his is the lesson: Never give in. Never give in. Never, never, never, never—in nothing, great or small, large or petty—never give in, except to convictions of honour and good sense. Never yield to force. Never yield to the apparently overwhelming might of the enemy. We stood all alone a year ago, and to many countries it seemed that our account was closed, we were finished. All this tradition of ours, our songs, our School history, this part of the history of this country, were gone and finished and liquidated. Very different is the mood today. Britain, other nations thought, had drawn a sponge across her slate. But instead our country stood in the gap. There was no flinching and no thought of giving in; and by what seemed almost a miracle to those outside these Islands, though we ourselves never doubted it, we now find ourselves in a position where I say that we can be sure that we have only to persevere to conquer." (Winston Churchill) *Pathos, Ethos*

e) _____ "Remember no one can make you feel inferior without your consent." (Eleanor Roosevelt) *Pathos*

f) _____ "Love is the irresistible desire to be irresistibly desired." (Mark Twain) *Pathos*

g) _____ "We learned about honesty and integrity—that the truth matters . . . that you don't take shortcuts or play by your own set of rules . . . and success doesn't count unless you earn it fair and square." (Michelle Obama) *Ethos*

h) _____ "Stocks [have] been so much more attractive than bonds." (Warren Buffet) *Logos*

i) _____ "I am an American, not an Asian-American. My rejection of hypenation has been called race treachery, but it is really a demand that America delivers the promises of its dream to all citizens equally." (Bharati Mukherjee). *Ethos*

j) _____ "Everyone must dream. We dream to give ourselves hope. To stop dreaming . . .

That's like saying you can never change your fate. Isn't that true?" (Amy Tan) *Pathos*

## EXERCISE 3: CHAPTER. 4

Determine which logical fallacy is best exemplified in the following statements:

1. _____Either we require children to exercise several times each week in physical education class, or we watch a firm increase in children who are earning low grades and dropping out of school. *false dilemma*

2. _____A lifestyle that does not include exercise must cause diabetes because a higher percentage of people who do not exercise are diagnosed with diabetes than active people. *post hoc, ergo proctor hoc*

3. _____Exercising irregularly does not lead to a shorter lifespan because my grandmother did not exercise, and she lived until 86. *statistics of small numbers*

4. _____The National Institute of Health (N.I.H.) has an obligation to provide free exercise opportunities for everyone because people without access to gyms have a right to resources provided by the government. *circular argument*

5. _____If the United States does not adopt a socialist medical plan, more citizens will move to Canada so they can afford health care for their families. *slippery slope*

6. _____If people do not exercise regularly and get enough sleep, they will risk dying prematurely. *pathos*

7. _____Everyone in the neighborhood is joining the local gym, "Get Fit Today!"; therefore, we should join also since our neighbors are losing weight. *bandwagon*

8. _____Mr. Kingston, our physical education teacher, endorses Vitamin D as the most important vitamin an adult should take every day. Look what taking Vitamin D has done for him: greater vitality and rides his bike to his office. *appeal to false authority*

9. _____ Physical activity helps to reduce body fat by improving the body's ability to burn calories. People who increase their exercise can now eat larger quantities of food. *non sequitur*

10. _____Since several people have become injured while rollerblading in the park, we should ban the sport in the local area. *pars pro toto*

## EXERCISE 1: CHAPTER 6

"Laugh and the world laughs with you" (Ella Wheeler Wilcox) _____*antanaclasis*

"We shall fight on the beaches, we shall fight on the landing grounds, we shall fight on the fields and in the streets, we shall fight in the hills" (Winston Churchill). _____*anaphora*

"Progress is neither proclamation nor palaver. It is not pretense nor play on prejudice. It is not the perturbation of the people passion-wrought, nor a promise proposed" (Warren G. Harding)._____ _____*alliteration*

"Rome has spoken; the case is concluded" (St. Augustine). _____*personification*

"Her voice is full of money" (F. Scott Fitzgerald)._____ *metonymy*

"A cathedral, a wave of a storm, a dancer's leap, never turn out to be as high as we had hoped" (Marcel Proust). _____ *asyndeton*

"Unless hours were cups of sack, and minutes capons, and clocks the tongues of bawds, and dials the signs of leaping houses, and the blessed sun himself a fair hot wench in flame-color'd taffeta, I see no reason why thou shouldst be so superfluous to demand the time of day" (Shakespeare, *Hamlet*, IV. 1.2.7)._____*polysyndeton*

"But passion lends them power, time means, to meet" (Shakespeare, *Romeo and Juliet*, II. Prol. 13). _____*zeugma*

"From such crooked wood as that which man is made of, nothing straight can be fashioned" (Immanuel Kant)._____ *hyperbaton*

"Was this the face that launched a thousand ships/ And burnt the topless towers of Ilium"? (Christopher Marlowe)._____*synecdoche*

"Love is an irresistible desire to be irresistibly desired" (Robert Frost). _____*polyptoton*

"She was not quite what you would call refined. She was not quite what you would call unrefined. She was the kind of person that keeps a parrot" (Mark Twain)._____ *anaphora*

"Why I should fear I know not/Since guiltiness I know not; but yet I feel I fear" (Shakespeare, *Othello*, 5.2.38)._____ _____ *epistrophe*

"If thou hast any sound, or use of voice/Speak to me./ If there be any good thing to be done/That may to thee do ease and grace to me/Speak to me" (Shakespeare, *Hamlet*, 1.1.128)._____*symploce*

"A man may devote himself to death and destruction to save a nation; but no nation will devote itself to death and destruction to save mankind" (Samuel Taylor Coleridge)._____*antimetabole*

"He [von Stauffenberg, a leader for the plot] was the man who unmistakably wore the mantle of a near-mystic German past, a warrior Germany, a noble Germany, a poetic Germany, a Germany of myth and longing" (Justin Cartwright). _____*antanaclasis*

## EXERCISE 4: CHAPTER 6

Which type of sentence (loose or periodic) is exhibited below? *periodic*

"And the letter had broken my father's heart so much—these daughters calling my mother from another life he never knew—that he gave the letter to my mother's old friend Auntie Lindo and asked her to write back and tell my sisters, in the greatest way possible, that my mother was dead" (Amy Tan).

## EXERCISE 6: CHAPTER 6

Label types of sentences (Simple, Compound, Complex, or Compound-Complex) in excerpt:

"Work-Life Balance Is a Myth. Do This Instead" by Marcus Buckingham and Ashley Goodall

It seems more useful, then, to not try to balance the unbalanceable, but to treat work the same way you do life: By maximizing what you love. *compound-complex* Here's what we mean. *simple* Consider why two people doing exactly the same work seem to gain strength and joy from very different moments. *simple* When we interviewed several anesthesiologists, we found that while their title and job function are identical, the thrills and chills they feel in their job are not. *compound-complex* One said he loved the thrill of holding each patient hovering at that one precise point between life and death, while he shuddered at the "pressure" of helping each patient get healthy once the operation was complete. *complex* Another said she loved the bedside conversations before the operation, and the calm sensitivity required to bring a sedated patient gently back to consciousness without the panic that afflicts many patients. *compound*

Another was drawn mostly to the intricacies of the anesthetic mechanism itself and has dedicated herself to defining precisely how each drug does what it does. *simple* Each one of us, for no good reason other than the clash of our chromosomes, draws strength from different activities, situations, moments, and interactions. *complex*

## EXERCISE 8: CHAPTER 6

Identify the types of openings: Phrases or Clauses—adverbial, adjectival, appositive, infinitive, preposition, or participial—in sentences from literary authors:

_____ *"Although they lived in style,* they felt always an anxiety in the house" (D. H. Lawrence). *Adverbial*

_____ "the watching, listening faces underwent a change, the eyes focusing on something within; the music seemed to soothe a poison out of the" (James Baldwin). *Adjectival*

_____Rachel Carson, *a biologist and writer*, published the novel *Silent Spring* in 1962. *Appositive*

_____ *"To err* is human; to forgive, divine" (*Alexander Pope*). *Infinitive*

_____ *"On the pleasant shore off the French Riviera, about halfway between Marseilles and the Italian border* stands a large, proud, rose-colored hotel" (F. Scott Fitzgerald). *Prepositional*

_____ *"Whirling happily in my starchy frock, showing off my biscuit-polished patent-leather shoes and lavender socks, tossing my head in a way that makes my ribbons bounce,* I stand, hands on hips, before my father" (Alice Walker). *Participial*

## *EXERCISE 1:* CHAPTER 7

Circle verbs, and label as transitive or intransitive:

The director *blocked* [T] the actors' movements for a particularly dramatic scene.

Due to her aching shoulder, Alison *delegated* [T] her presentation to a coworker.

Recently, Taylor *traveled* [IT] to Alaska to photograph the wildlife and mountains.

*Reciting* [T] their poems from memory, each poet *performed* [IT] superbly.

## EXERCISE 1: CHAPTER 8

Note below if the following texts are scholarly or nonscholarly:

_____ "Is criminal behavior a central component of psychopathy? Conceptual directions for resolving the debate" by Jennifer Skeem and David J. Cooke in *Psychological Assessment* journal. *scholarly*

_____*Einstein: His Life and Universe* by Walter Isaacson *scholarly*

_____ *Rocket Girl: The Story of Mary Sherman Morgan, America's First Female Rocket Scientist* by George D. Morgan *scholarly*

_____*Time* magazine *nonscholarly*

_____*Tampa Bay Times* newspaper *nonscholarly*

_____*GQ* magazine *nonscholarly*

## EXERCISE 2: CHAPTER 8

Note below if the following are primary or secondary texts, or both:

_____*War Letters* by Andrew Carroll (collection of authentic letters written to and from soldiers and their loved ones during Civil Wars—Persian Gulf Wars) *primary*

_____*World Religions: Origins History Practices Beliefs Worldview* by Franjo Terhart and Janina Schulze, writers and scholars of religion. *primary*

_____ *A Collection of Sermons Given in Paris c. 1267, Including a New Text by Saint Bonaventura on the Life of Saint Francis* by Robert E. Lerner who offers commentary about the sermons and provides digitized copies of the original sermons. *primary*

_____ "College students' prevalence and perceptions of text messaging while driving" by Marissa Harrison who reports findings of study in *Accident Analysis & Prevention* journal. *secondary*

_____"Sun and Wind Alter Global Landscape, Leaving Utilities Behind" by Justin Gillis who reports on topic in *The New York Times. secondary*

_____*Amazing Grace*—a film based on true events featuring William Wilberforce, an English politician who seeks to abolish slavery in Britain in the face of major opposition in the 1700s. *secondary*

_____*Beowulf: A Translation and Commentary* by Christopher Tolkien and J.R.R. Tolkien. *secondary*

## GRAMMAR, PUNCTUATION, AND USAGES EXERCISES CHAPTER 9

Answer Keys
*Exercises A–F used with Permission from Mary Mocsary—English Professor,
Southeastern Louisiana University.

## EXERCISE 1: CHAPTER 9 COMMAS

Directions: Add commas where necessary in the sentences. There may be sentences that do not require commas.

1. When we watched the film, everyone was silent and riveted.
2. We telephoned the diplomatic center, and we reached a representative promptly.
3. We telephoned the diplomatic center and reached a representative promptly.
4. For example, people are living on the streets because they cannot make ends meet.
5. On the street corner, there was always a man who would beg me for money, and he would talk about religion.
6. I joined the military, specifically the Coast Guard, because I can make an impact on the world.
7. Mary Shelley's novel, *Frankenstein* or the *Modern Prometheus*, was first published in 1818.
8. We participated in the summer program; therefore, we may have a higher chance of acceptance at the liberal arts college.
9. Though the football game was terribly exciting, the outcome was overshadowed by the brawl among temperamental players.
10. We watched the game on our new HD television and ate a lot of junk food.

11. We wanted the Midwestern team to win because we are longtime residents of Illinois.
12. We look forward to the Super bowl, and we plan to host a game party that day.
13. In Homer's epic narrative, the hero Odysseus, faces many dangers such as the god Poseidon, the Sirens, and the goddess Calypso.
14. The base of the Statue of Liberty is granite, but the igneous rock is from Stony Creek, Connecticut.
15. When we prepared for backpacking trip across Europe, we packed extra socks, soap, and phone chargers.

## EXERCISE 2: CHAPTER 9 ADVERB CLAUSES AND COMMA USAGE

* Adverb clauses answer the questions: How? When? Where? To What Extent?
* Adverb clauses contain: subordinating conjunctions, subjects, and verbs.

Subordinating conjunctions include when, if, because, although, since, while, before, after, unless

* When the adverb clause appears at the beginning of the sentence, add a comma:
    Ex. When I arrive at the dormitory, I will meet my new roommate. (#1)
* When the adverb clause appears at the end of the sentence, do not add a comma.
    Ex. I will meet my new roommate when I arrive at the dormitory. (#2)

Directions: Referring to the comma rules above, add commas in the following sentences where necessary. Label each sentence with #1 if the clause is in the first part of the sentence or with #2 if the clause is in the second part of the sentence.

1. I usually have coffee after I wake up in the morning._____ #2
2. If I have homework I'll finish it after dinner in Rockman Library._____ #1
3. When I finish my homework I usually read a Science Fiction book for pleasure._____#1
4. I often listen to music only on my iPhone though I have many CDs._____ #2
5. I read in bed because reading helps me fall asleep._____#2

6. Before I take an exam I reread my notes and do practice formulas._____#1
7. While I finished my laundry, I completed my lab report and studied for my Introduction to Psychology exam._____#1
8. Since we have a fall break we are traveling to Vermont to see the foliage._____#1
9. I hurry to Chemistry class in Taylor Hall because the transitions between classes are only 10 minutes._____#2
10. Unless there is a lot of snow and sleet on the roads the school will open tomorrow._____#1

## EXERCISE 3: CHAPTER 9 COMMAS AND SEMICOLONS FOR COMPOUND SENTENCES

Rules for commas and semicolons for compound sentences:

a. Joined by comma and coordinating conjunction: fanboys: for, and, nor, boy, or, yet, so
    Ex. We are flying to Colorado for the holidays, and we plan to ski in Aspen.
b. Joined with semicolon
    Ex. We are flying to Colorado for the holidays; we plan to ski in Aspen.
c. Joined with semicolon, subordinating conjunction, comma
    Subordinating Conjunctions: as a result, consequently, for example, however, in fact, nevertheless, therefore
    Ex. We are flying to Colorado for the holidays; however, we can stay only a few days.

*Exercise*
Directions: For each compound sentence, punctuate using one of the above choices (a, b, or c)

1. The ski club members have skied in New Hampshire_____they enjoyed the beautiful scenery of the White Mountains. options: . . ; . . . , and
2. Snowboarding in Vermont is a fun way to spend winter break_____ our budget allows us to stay for the whole week. options: . . . ; . . . .,and
3. We found some inexpensive lodging and skiing packages_____ the Stowe Lodge offers the best deal for students. options: . . . ;however, . . . , yet
4. In addition to skiing, we hiked the trails around Aspen_____ we ate at a few smokehouse restaurants. options: . . . ; . . . , and

5. Skiers and snowboarders are particular about conditions_____ they prefer either ice or powdery snow_____ but not both. options: . . . ; . . . ., but . . . , and . . . ,

## *EXERCISE 4:*
## CHAPTER *9 CAPITALIZATION*

Directions: Capitalize all relevant titles, names, locations, and other proper nouns.

1. After leaving his house, Jeremy headed Northwest toward the movie theater to see *Harry Potter and the Sorcerer Stone.*
2. Since I ran out of ink for the printer, I had to drive during a freezing winter day to buy cartridges. *none*
3. Though it was a very cold winter day, Juanita went for a run and felt invigorated.
4. Although there have been extraordinary figures in world literature, people consider Homer and Shakespeare two of the greatest authors to have ever graced this earth.
5. People often think that the Battle of Gettysburg was the bloodiest in the Civil War; however, the Battle of Antietam claims this fact.
6. Even though it is widely considered the toughest course, I wanted to take Professor Adam's English and Professor Torok's Multi-Variable Calculus II courses.
7. When I took a religion class, we studied the bible, the Koran, and the Torah to compare the virtues of each holy work.
8. Problems in the Middle East escalated today due to a bombing of a local oil pipeline.
9. Senator Howard's campaign is in full force thanks to her team who work in the Rayburn building on Independence Avenue in the Southwest area of Washington D.C.
10. My nephew, C.J., is a sophomore at Purdue University in West Lafayette, Indiana.
11. The U.S. Coast Guard conducted a successful operation for which its Florida crew received praise from the National Transportation Safety Board.
12. *The Scarlet Letter, The Great Gatsby, The Color Purple*, and *Her Eyes Were Watching God* are several of the most common novels in American high school English curriculums.

13. We could not decide if we wanted to buy a Mac Pro or Dell computer to play *Batman: Arkham Knight and Destin* video games.

## *EXERCISE 5:*
## CHAPTER *9 PUNCTUATING TITLES OF LITERATURE*

1. I searched *Netflix* and found a British series, *Broadchurch*, which is a crime drama about a young boy murdered in a small town, and everyone is a suspect.
2. In high school English class, we read *The Great Gatsby* by F. Scott Fitzgerald and *Beloved* by Toni Morrison.
3. In college English class, we read Maya Angelou's poem "Phenomenal Woman" and Homer's epic poem, *The Odyssey*.
4. Have you read the article, "French Police Destroys Virus that Hit Nearly 1 Million Computers," in *Time* magazine?
5. We joined the millions of people who subscribe to *Amazon Prime* to watch old films such as *The Godfather* series and *Apocalypse Now*.
6. My favorite episode of The Lord of the Rings is The Return of the King.
7. Bruno Mars won a Grammy award for his album, *24K Magic*, which includes songs: "24K Magic, Perm, and Finesse."
8. Paula found an article, "Biochemical Breakthroughs in the 21$^{st}$ Century," in the database, *EBSCO*.
9. We watched the *Geico* commercial entitled: "More Insurance for Less Money."
10. Most college freshmen have read Faulkner's short story, "A Rose for Emily."

### REFERENCE LIST OF FIFTEEN COMMON ERRORS IN GRAMMAR AND USAGE

(a = incorrect; b = correct)
Use "who" directly after noun referring to people.
1a. Lawmakers *that* can produce legislature that increases the sustainability of the American food industry.
1b. Lawmakers *who* can produce legislature that increases the sustainability of the American food industry have a place on the itinerary.

Use professional diction in academic writing.

2a. *It talks about* how the act came to be and what it does.

2b. *The author* explained how the Act originated and functioned.

Use variation in opener of sentences; avoid starting too many sentences with demonstrative pronouns (That, These, This, Those) or with "What" unless starting a question.

3a. *This* shows the writer's view of space exploration.

3b. *Demonstrating* the writer's view of space exploration, the argument holds credibility.

3c. *What* is seen to one person as clear is not to another person due to differences.

3d. *What* is the meaning of Keats' poem "Ode on a Grecian Urn"?

Use "Since" or "Due to" instead of "Because" to begin sentences.

4a. *Because* we were stranded at the airport, we ate dinner in the food court.

4b. *Since* we were stranded at the airport, we ate dinner in the food court.

Use historical present tense instead of past tense when writing about literature. This tense "brings alive" the text into the present time.

5a. Incorrect: In Shakespeare's comedy *Twelfth Night*, there *were* twins who *became* separated after a shipwreck.

5b. Correct: The twins, Viola and Sebastian, *become* part of a mixed-up love plot that *features* a count and a countess.

Use specific words instead of "it."

6a. *It* meant that the land was so barren and dangerous that it was almost magnificent.

6b. In particular, the *photo* reflected land so barren and dangerous that it was almost magnificent.

6c. *It* may bring about effective communication.

6d. *Analysis* of conversations between men and women may result in more effective communication between the opposite sexes.

Use "who" as a subject and "whom" as an object (preposition or direct); to judge if you use "who" replace with "I, we, he, she, or they"; for "whom," replace with "me, him, her, us, or them." Ex. Who [He] is driving to the game? To whom [him] should I address this letter?

7a. Incorrect: To *Who* This May Concern

7b. Correct: To *Whom* This May Concern

Incorrect: Military members are those *whom* live by core values.

Correct: Military members are those *who* live by core values.

Use consistent historical present tense—provides an immediacy to the reading experience of timeless literature.

8a. Incorrect: In this tragedy, Romeo *fell* in love with Juliet, but their families *hated* each other.

8b. Correct: In this tragedy, Romeo *falls* in love with Juliet, but their families *hate* each other.

Avoid using contractions in academic writing.

9a. Incorrect: I *didn't* realize that I could have such an impact on one person's life.

9b. Correct: I *did not* realize that I could have such an impact on one person's life.

Avoid mixing pronouns in the same sentence.

10a. Incorrect: *Their* diplomas symbolize dedication and achievement to *one's* studies.

10b. *Their* diplomas symbolize dedication and achievement to *their* studies.

Use a dash between double adjectives which both describe a common noun.

11a. Incorrect: Last Thursday, students attended a *well organized* art show on campus.

11b. Correct: Last year, students attended a *well-organized* art show on campus.

When no citation exists after a sentence, place a period or comma inside the quotations.

12a. Incorrect: The administrative assistant referred to the visitor as a *"Jacob"*.

12b. Correct: The administrative assistant referred to the visitor as a *"Jacob."*

Incorrect: Even though they are referred to as *"freshmen"*, the fraternity brothers treated them as friends.

Correct: Even though they are referred to as *"freshmen,"* the fraternity brothers treated them as friends.

Use "I feel, I believe, and I know" accurately. "I feel" is followed by an emotion. "I believe" and "I know" are followed by an assertion.

13a. Incorrect: *I feel* like we are not communicating well.

13b. Correct: *I feel* sad that we are not communicating well.

Incorrect: *I feel* that children should not be over-medicated.

Correct: *I believe* children should not be over-medicated.

13c. Incorrect: *I feel* we spent a lot of money during December.

13d. Correct: *I know* we spent a lot of money during December.

Use apostrophes after years only when showing possession.

14a. Incorrect: My parents love the music of the *1960's.*

14b. Correct: My parents love *1960's* music.

Use "should have, could have, would have" instead of "should of, could of, would of."

15a. Incorrect: James and Colin *should of* paid for their tickets earlier.

15b. Correct: James and Colin *should have* paid for their tickets earlier.

## *EXERCISE 6:* REFERENCE LIST OF FIFTEEN COMMON ERRORS IN GRAMMAR AND USAGE

Directions: Choose the correct word in the parentheses. Refer to the "Reference List of 20 Common Errors in Grammar and Usage." Answers will vary, unless otherwise corrected.

1. Delete "it" and rewrite this sentence using higher-level diction:

    It is a shorter time between Thanksgiving and Christmas this year, but we'll deal with it.

2. Replace the casual language with academic language in this sentence:

    Zora Neale, Hurston, in her novel *Their Eyes Are Watching God*, talks about a girl who ends up becoming a woman in charge of her destiny.

3. Choose the correct word—who (subject; replace with "he, she, or they" to verify) or whom (object of preposition; replace with "him, her, or them" to verify)—for the following sentences:

    We filled care packages for the troops (who/whom) will not come home for the holidays.

    For (who/whom) do we label these care packages?

    Lt. White is the officer (who/whom) the commander selected for the award.

4. Substitute appropriate pronouns (and make them consistent) in the following sentences:

    Authors of articles in *Psychology Today* make you feel like you're are a subject in the experiments.

    During student orientation, each freshman should register for their classes and submit one's financial form.

5. Place periods inside quotations without citations in these sentences:

    All of the college-bound students have heard the old saying, "Watch out for the freshman 10"

    A well-regarded author, Scott King, will speak during the "happy hour."

6. Use "I feel," "I believe," and "I know" (present or past tense) accurately in these sentences:

    _____relieved after receiving news about my grandmother's heart surgery.

    _____there is a human trafficking problem in India.

    _____in the rights of animals who cannot speak for themselves.

7. Correct phrases that begin with "should," "could," or "would" (use "have" instead of "of") in these sentences:

    The opposing team could of won the state championship if there were not so many injuries.

    We should of arrived early to sit in the first row.

8. Rephrase the openings to these sentences to avoid starting sentences with: Because, What—unless starting

    a question, and There (often overused along with This and That).

    Because we only have ten days until finals week we should start studying for our exams.

    What I mean is that the government should spend more money on space exploration.

    This site is where we bought gifts and sent them several weeks in advance of Hanukkah.

9. Avoid slang, overused words and phrases (ex. being, ended up, and things) in your academic writing.

    Being that it is July, swabs ended up doing drill and other things indoors, and they felt faint because it was still so hot in Rolanda Hall.

    Since it is very warm in July, swabs completed a drill and other exercises in Rolanda Hall, even though they still felt faint because the gym was not much cooler.

10. Add dashes where necessary in the following sentence:

    We decided to buy a well functioning, refurbished laptop for a low price.

11. Choose the correct word in the following sentence:

    Students (that/who) eat nutritionally and run twenty miles per week are the definition of "fitness."

12. Correct apostrophes in the following sentence:

Kim's parents listen to music from the 1970's.
The patent on the invention was circa early 2000's.

## *EXERCISE 6*: GRAMMAR AND USAGE ANSWER KEY

Directions: Choose the correct word in the parentheses. Refer to the "Reference List of 20 Common Errors in Grammar and Usage" Answers will vary, unless otherwise corrected.

Delete "it" and rewrite this sentence using higher-level diction

It is a shorter time between Thanksgiving and Christmas this year, but we'll deal with it.

1. Replace the casual language with academic language in this sentence:

Zora Neale, Hurston, in her novel *Their Eyes Are Watching God*, talks about a girl who ends up becoming a woman in charge of her destiny.

2. Choose the correct word—who (subject; replace with "he, she, or they" to verify) or whom (object of preposition; replace with "him, her, or them" to verify)—for the following sentences:

We filled care packages for the troops (who/whom) will not come home for the holidays.

For (who/whom) do we label these care packages?

Lt. White is the officer (who/whom) the commander selected for the award.

3. Substitute appropriate pronouns (and make them consistent) in the following sentences:

Authors of articles in *Psychology Today* make you feel like students you're are a subject in the experiments.

During student orientation, each freshman should register for their classes and submit his/her financial form.

4. Place periods inside quotations without citations in these sentences:

All of the college-bound students have heard the old saying, "Watch out for the freshman 10."

A well-regarded author, Scott King, will speak during the "happy hour."

5. Use "I feel," "I believe," and "I know" (present or past tense) accurately in these sentences:

*I felt* relieved after receiving news about my grandmother's heart surgery.

*I know* there is a human trafficking problem in India.

*I believe* in the rights of animals who cannot speak for themselves.

6. Correct phrases that begin with "should," "could," or "would" (use "have" instead of "of") in these sentences:

The opposing team *could have* won the state championship if there were not so many injuries.

We *should have* arrived early to sit in the first row.

7. Rephrase the openings to these sentences to avoid starting sentences with: Because, What—unless starting a question, and There (often overused along with This and That).

Because we only have ten days until finals week we should start studying for our exams.

What I mean is that the government should spend more money on space exploration.

This site is where we bought gifts and sent them several weeks in advance of Hanukkah.

8. Avoid slang, overused words and phrases (ex. being, ended up, and things) in your academic writing.

Being that it is July, swabs ended up doing drill and other things indoors, and they felt faint because it was still so hot in Rolanda Hall.

Since it is very warm in July, swabs completed a drill and other exercises in Rolanda Hall, even though they still felt faint because the gym was not much cooler.

9. Add dashes where necessary in the following sentence:

We decided to buy a well-functioning, refurbished laptop for a low price.

10. Choose the correct word in the following sentence:

Students (that/*who*) eat nutritionally and run twenty miles per week are the definition of "fitness."

11. Correct apostrophes in the following sentence:

Kim's parents listen to music from the *1970s*.

The patent on the invention was circa early *2000s*.

## REFERENCE LIST OF
## SPELLING AND USAGE

1. accept-except Caroline *accepts* feedback from everyone *except* her family.
2. affect-effect The *effect* of the new financial-aid policy *affects* many students.
3. all ready-already We were *all ready* to leave at 5:00 p.m. only to realize the bus had departed *already*.
4. between-among *Between* you and me, we have 60 apps *among* the icons on our cell phones.
5. capitol-capital We drove through Richmond, the *capital* of Virginia, on our way to Washington D.C. to visit the *Capitol* building.
6. choose-chose Ray *chose* the entrée instead of the meal that other customers *choose* regularly.
7. cite-sight-site After looking at the *Credo site* online, I *cited* an ophthalmology journal article about the gift of *sight* for several blind children.
8. each other Some members of our high-school class have not seen *one another*.

    one another My best friend and I see *each other* fairly often.
9. farther-further I want to discuss the issue *further* before we drive any *farther* to the beach.
10. fewer-less In regular yogurt, there are *fewer* calories than one might expect.

    In the refrigerator, there is *less* milk than I expected.

    $\geq \leq$ There is *less than* a 20 percent chance of snow tomorrow.

    There is greater than an 80 percent chance of snow tomorrow.
11. forth-fourth Come *forth* and receive your *fourth* award at the ceremony.
12. it's-its *It's* foolish to drive a car to *its* speed capacity unless you are driving on the *Autobahn* in Germany.
13. lie-lay Angela *lies* down in the afternoon while Quinton *lays* the new tiles.
14. led-lead Martina *led* the troops, shouting, "Get the *lead* out of your boots!"
15. lose-loose Did you *lose* your bracelet because the clasp was too *loose*?
16. past-passed In the *past*, Carlos *passed* all of his exams.
17. precede-proceed The graduation keynote's speech *preceded* the president giving diplomas to graduates as they *proceeded* across the stage.
18. principal-principle Mrs. Cooper, our school *principal*, is a person of high *principles*.
19. though-thorough *Though* Kelly tried hard, she did not do a *thorough* job of cleaning.
20. through-threw They were caught wandering *through* the mall after hours; therefore, the security team *threw* them out.
21. their-there *Their* textbooks are *there*, on the table.
22. then-than Since *then*, I like Mexican food better *than* Chinese food.
23. two-too-to For *two* days, it has been *too* cold *to* ski.
24. whether-weather I wonder *whether* the gas supply will be sufficient for the cold *weather*.
25. were-we're They *were* taking the exams yesterday, and *we're* going to do the same today.
26. where-wear We wondered *where* we could play golf and what to *wear* on the course.
27. which-witch *Which* woman is a real *witch* living in Salem, Massachusetts?
28. whose-who's *Who's* the person *whose* keys are missing?
29. who-whom *Who* is the new Dean of Students with *whom* you will work this fall?
30. you're-your *You're* allowed into the concert after purchasing *your* tickets.

### *EXERCISE 7*: REFERENCE LIST OF SPELLING AND USAGE

For each sentence, choose the correct word in each set.

1. I remembered everything (accept/except) my sunglasses, which did not cause (too, to, two) much stress since I had an extra pair in the car.
2. We turned on the music as we (passed/past) the mall, (then/than) turned right onto Pearl St. where the optometrist's office is located.
3. (Between/Among) you and me, you can share your feelings. (Their/there) is nothing you have to hold back from us.
4. I think it's a (capitol/capital) idea to see the new Egyptian exhibit at the museum (You're/your) going to regret not seeing this magnificent (cite, site, sight).
5. I hope you (choose/chose) the right movie at the theater because (we're/were) lost in this downtown area, and the show has (all ready, already) begun.

6. The (farther/further) we hike up the path, the (fewer/less) the chances for us to hike back to our car before dark.

7. My little Shiatsu Bruno, (who, whom, which) I love, was a that stray we adopted.

8. (It's/its) always polite to address a letter "To (Who/Whom) This May Concern."

10. Mark had to (lie/lay) new pipes, because the old ones were made of (lead/led).

11. (Who/Whom) was the one pulled the dog by (its/it's) tail?

12. Since the quarterback's shoelaces were (lose/loose), he fumbled the ball in the muddy (weather/whether).

13. The electric bill was (past/passed) due (which/witch) caused the power cut off at Jamie's house.

14. As the (principal/principle) writer of the annual report, Mrs. Harriman knew better (then/than) presenting something substandard to the shareholders.

15. The basketball player (through-threw) the ball in the basket for a three-pointer, but it was not enough, and his team would (lose/loose) by five points.

16. Our team members lean on (each other, one another) for support on the field. Two opposing coaches talked to (each other, one another) after the game.

17. High winds and hail (affected, effected) our flight to Arizona. The (affect, effect) was a longer layover in Chicago.

18. It's (two/too/to) expensive (two/too/to) visit the amusement park for (two/too/to) days straight.

19. We (were/we're) all surprised when bird flew (forth/fourth) into the house during the rainstorm.

20. I wonder (who/whom) knows the correct style format to (cite, sight, site) this library database.

## *EXERCISE 7*: REFERENCE LIST OF SPELLING AND USAGE ANSWER KEY

Using the "Reference List of Spelling and Usage," choose the correct word in the parentheses for each sentence.

1. I remembered everything (accept/*except*) my sunglasses, which did not cause (*too*, to, two) much stress since I had an extra pair in the car.

2. We turned on the music as we (*passed*/past) the mall, (*then*/than) turned right onto Pearl St. where the optometrist's office is located.

3. (*Between*/Among) you and me, you can share your feelings. (Their/*There*) is nothing you have to hold back from us.

4. I think it's a (capitol/*capital*) idea to see the new Egyptian exhibit at the museum (*You're*/your) going to regret not seeing this magnificent (cite, *site*, sight).

5. I hope you (choose/*chose*) the best movie at the theater because (*we're*/were) lost in this downtown area, and the show has (all ready, *already*) begun.

6. The (*farther*/further) we hike up the path, the (fewer/*less*) food we will have for this adventure.

7. My little Shiatsu Bruno, (who, *whom*, which) I love, was a that stray we adopted.

8. (*It's*/Its) always polite to address a letter "To (Who/*Whom*) This May Concern."

9. Mark had to (lie/*lay*) new pipes, because the old ones were made of (*lead*/led).

10. (*Who*/Whom) was the one pulled the dog by (*its*/it's) tail?

11. Since the quarterback's shoelaces were (lose/*loose*), he fumbled the ball in the muddy (weather/whether).

12. The electric bill was (*past*/passed) due, (*which*/witch) caused the power cut off at Jamie's house.

13. As the (principal/*principle*) writer of the annual report, Mrs. Harriman knew better (then/*than*) presenting something substandard to the shareholders.

14. The basketball player (through/*threw*) the ball in the basket for a three-pointer, but it was not enough, and his team would (lose/loose) by five points.

15. Our team members lean on (each other, *one another*) for support on the field. Two opposing coaches talked to (*each other*, one another) after the game.

16. High winds and hail (*affected*, effected) our flight to Arizona. The (affect, *effect*) was a longer layover in Chicago.

17. It's (two/*too*/to) expensive (two/too/*to*) visit the amusement park for (two/too/to) days straight.

18. We (*were*/we're) all surprised when bird flew (*forth*/fourth) into the house during the rainstorm.

20. I wonder (*who*/whom) knows the correct style format to (*cite*, sight, site) this library database.

# Works Cited

2 Live Crew. "Pretty Woman." *As Clean as They Wanna Be*. Skywalker Records, 1989. CD.

Anthony, Susan B. "On Women's Right to Vote." TheHistoryPlace.com. Web. 8 August 2015.

Aristotle. *Aristotle on Rhetoric: A Theory of Civic Discourse*. George Kennedy, ed. New York: Oxford UP, 1991. Print.

Beam, Christopher. "[Best] Film Ever!!!' How Do Movie Blurbs Work?" *Slate*. 25 November 2009.

Bernanke, Ben S. "The Economic Outlook and Monetary Policy." Federal Reserve Bank of Kansas City Economic Symposium. Jackson Hole, Wyoming. Federalreserve.gov. Web. 8 August 2014.

"The Birth of Mount Rushmore." *History Channel*. http://www.history.com/topics/us-presidents/mount-rushmore.

Bitzer, Lloyd. "The Rhetorical Situation." *Philosophy and Rhetoric* 1.1 (1968): 1–14.

"Black Hawk Pilot Michael Durant Writes from Captivity in Somalia to Assure His Wife and One-Year-Old-Son That, Although Injured, He is Still Alive." *War Letters: Extraordinary Correspondence from American Wars*. Andrew Carroll, ed. New York: Scribner, 2001: 467–468.

Blige, Mary J. "No More Drama." *No More Drama*. 2001. CD.

"Bloom's Taxonomy." Bloom's Taxonomy.org. Web. 8 August 2014.

Bowie, David. "Under Pressure." Queen. *Hot Space*. EMI, 1981. CD.

Boylanda, Emma J., et al. "Beyond-brand Effect of Television (TV) Food Advertisements/Commercials on Caloric Intake and Food Choice of 5–7-Year-Old Children." *Science Direct* 49.1 (2007): 263–267. Print.

Buckingham, Marcus and Ashley Goodall. "Work-Life Balance is a Myth. Do this Instead." 6 June 2019. https://time.com /5601671/work-life-balance-advice-love-loathe/.

Buckley, Jr. William F. "Why Don't We Complain?" *50 Essays*. Samuel Cohen, ed. New York: Bedford/St. Martin's, 2004: 64–70.

Carroll, Andrew, ed. *Operation Homecoming: Iraq, Afghanistan, and the Home Front, in the Words of U.S. Troops and Their Families*. Chicago: University of Chicago, 2008. Print.

Churchill, Winston. "Never Give In." *The Unrelenting Struggle: War Speeches by the Right Hon Winston Churchill*. 2nd ed. Charles Eade, ed. New York: Book for Libraries, 1971. Print.

Crichton, Michael. *Jurassic Park*. New York: Random House, 1990.

Dahiya, Monica Balyan. "Quest for the Past in an Alien Land: A Study of Jhumpa Lahiri's Namesake and Bharati Mukherjee's Jasmine." *Language In India*. July 2012: 497. Literature Resource Center. Web. 29 September 2014.

De Vorzon, Barry, and Perry Botkin, Jr. "Nadia's Theme." *Nadia's Theme (The Young and the Restless)*. A&M Records, 1976. Vinyl.

DiNicolantonio, James, and Sean Lucan. "Sugar Season. It's Everywhere, and Addictive." *The New York Times*. 22 December 2014. Web. 23 December 2014.

DiProperzio, Linda. "The Power of Birth Order." *Parents Magazine*. Parents.com. 27 October 2010. Web. 15 September 2015.

Edwards, Bernard, and Nile Rogers. *Good Times*. Chic. *Risqué*. Atlantic, 1979. Vinyl.

Elkind, David. "Playtime Is Over." *New York Times*. 26 March 2006: A19. Print.

Fenty, Robyn Rhianna. "SOS." *A Girl Like Me*. Universal Music International Div. 2006. CD.

Flesch, Rudolph. "The Flesch Reading Ease Ability Formula." *My Byline Media*, n.d. Web. 28 December 2014.

Fox, Maggie, and Erika Edwards. "Let Them Sleep In: Docs Want Later School Times for Teens." *NBC News*. 25 August 2014. Web. 15 September 2014.

Friedman, Thomas L. *The World is Flat: A Brief History of the Twenty-First Century*. New York: Farrar, Straus, and Giroux, 2005.

Gillis, Justin. "Sun and Wind Alter Global Landscape, Leaving Utilities Behind." *New York Times*. 14 September 2014: A1. Print.

Harball, Elizabeth and Climatewire. "As Carbon Dioxide Grows, Tropical Trees Do Not." *Scientific American*. 16 December 2014.

*Hardball Times. The Wall Street Opinion*. 29 August 2019. 25 May 2010 and updated 2 March 2018. Web. *Opposing Viewpoints*. https://www.opposingviews.com/sports/fay-vincent-gets-it-right-wrong.

Hemingway, Ernest. *The Old Man and the Sea*. New York: Scribner, 1952. Print.

Hemingway, Ernest. "Soldiers Home." *Ernest Hemingway: The Short Stories*. New York: Scribner Paperback Fiction Edition, 1995. Print.

Isaacson, Walter. *Steve Jobs*. New York: Simon and Schuster, 2011.

Johnson, Lyndon B. "We Shall Overcome." *Special Message to the Congress: The American Promise*. Washington, DC. 15 March 1965. Lbjlibrary.org. 15 September 2014.

Kilpatrick, Carroll. "Nixon Tells Editors, 'I'm Not a Crook'." *Washington Post*. 18 November 1975: n.p. Web. 8 August 2014.

Kohn, Alfie. *The Schools Our Children Deserve*. Boston: Houghton Mifflin, 1999. Print.

Konnikova, Maria. "What's Lost As Handwriting Fades?" *The New York Times*. 2 June 2014: D1. Print.

King, Martin Luther, Jr. "I Have a Dream." Washington, DC. 28 August 1963. Americanrhetoric.org. Web. 8 August 2014.

Lindenbaum, John. "Music Sampling and Copyright Law." Senior Thesis. Woodrow Wilson School of Public and International Affairs. Princeton University. April, 1999.

Madison, Lucy, and Sarah B. Boxer. "Mitt Romney: I like Being Able to Fire People for Bad Service." CBSNEWS.com. CBS. 9 January 2012. Web. 15 September 2014.

"Memory, Encoding Storage and Retrieval | Simply Psychology." *Simply Psychology*. Web. 15 September 2014.

Mystic Seaport Staff. "The Last Wooden Ship in the World." Mystic Seaport. n.p., n.d. Web. 15 September 2015.

National Geographic. "Earth." Web. 11 November 2014.

Nielson, Erik, and Charis E. Kubrin. "Rap Lyrics on Trial." *The New York Times*. 13 January 2014: A27. Print.

N.I.H. News in Health. *Health Capsule*. "Vaping Rises in Teens." 16 August 2019. Web. February 2019.

Obama, Barack. "Barack Obama's Acceptance Speech." Democratic Convention. americanrhetoric.org. 28 August 2008. Web.

Orbinson, Ray. "Pretty Woman." *The All-Time Greatest Hits of Ray Orbinson*. Monumental Records, 1972. Vinyl.

Orwell, George. "The Frontiers of Art and Propaganda" BBC. GB, London. 29 May 1941. Radio.

"Our Commitment to Recycling." *Apple.com*. Web. 8 January 2015.

Pendergrass, BobbyLou. "The Sister of Army Specialist Killed in Vietnam Asks President John F. Kennedy 'If a War is Worth Fighting—Isn't it Worth Fighting to Win?' and President John F. Kennedy Responds." *War Letters*: 391–392.

Perkins, Mitali. "A Note to Young Immigrants." Teachingtolerance.org. *Teaching Tolerance*. 1 Jan. 2005. Web. 15 September 2014.

Pew Research Center: Internet and Technology. "Social Media Fact Sheet." 12 June 2019. Web. 15 August 2019.

Pittman, Mathew and Brandon Reich. "Social Media and Loneliness: Why an Instagram Picture May Be Worth More than a Thousand Twitter Words." *Computers in Human Behavior* 62 (2016): 155–167. Print.

Proulx, Annie. "Inspiration? Head Down the Back Road, and Stop for the Yard Sales." *The Story and Its Writer: An Introduction*. 8th ed. Ann Charters, ed. New York: Bedford/St. Martin's, 2010.

Queneau, Raymond. *Exercises in Style*. Trans. Barbara Wright. New York: New Directions, 1981.

Rice, Condoleezza. *No Greater Honor: A Memoir of My Years in Washington*. New York: Random House, 2011.

Ringel, Faye. *Correct Paraphrase and Documentation: How to Avoid Plagiarism the Honor Offense for Academics*. Rev. 2012. TS. U.S. Coast Guard Academy.

Ripken, Cal Jr. "Cal Ripken Jr: Farewell to Baseball Address, October 6, 2001." *American Rhetoric: The Power of Oratory in the United States*. n.p., 6 October 2001. Web. 15 September 2014.

Scott, Brian. ReadabilityFormulas.com. "Readability Tools to Check for Reading Levels, Reading Assessment, and Reading Grade Levels." 2012. Web. 3 November 2014.

Shah, Anup. "Causes of Poverty." *Global Issues: Social, Political, Economic and Environmental Issues That Affect Us All*. Web. 28 September 2014.

Shane-Simpson, Christina, Adriana Manago, Naomi Gaggi, and Kristen Gillespie-Lynch. "Why Do College Students Prefer Facebook, Twitter or Instagram? Site Affordances, Tensions between Privacy and Self-Expression, and Implications for Social Capital." *Computers in Human Behavior* 86 (2018): 276–288. Print.

Smith, John. "From The General History." *Adventures in American Literature*. Deluzain et al. New York: Holt, Rinehart, and Winston, 1996, 16–21.

Smith, Will. "Men in Black." *Big Willie Style*. Columbia, 1997. CD.

"SOAPSTone: A Strategy for Reading and Writing." APCentral. College Board. https://apcentral.collegeboard.org/courses/resources/soapstone-strategy-reading-and-writing.

Soft Cell. "Tainted Love." Ed Cobb. *13 Going on 3*. Soundtrack. Hollywood, 2004. CD.

Specialist "Ski" Kolodziejski. "Personal Narrative." Specialist "Ski" Kolodziejski. *Operation Homecoming: Iraq, Afghanistan, and the Home Front, in the Words of U.S. Troops and Their Families*. Andrew Carroll, ed. New York: Random House, 2006.

Strunk, William. *The Elements of Style: The Original Edition*. New York: Soho Press, 2011. Originally printed: New York: Harcourt, 1923.

Sugarhill Gang. "Rapper's Delight." *Rappers Delight: Best of Sugarhill Gang*. Rhino, 1979. Vinyl.

Talbot, et al. "Sleep Deprivation in Adolescents and Adults: Change in Affect." *Emotion* 10.6 (December 2010): 831–841.

"Toulmin Method." Purdue University: Purdue Online Writing Lab. https://owl.purdue.edu/owl/general_writing/academic_writing/historical_perspectives_on_argumentation/toulmin_argument.html.

Vanilla Ice. "Ice Ice Baby." *Hooked*. Ultra Records, 1989. Vinyl.

Vincent, Fay. "Doping Has No Place in Sports." *The Wall Street Journal*. 29 August 2019. *Opposing Viewpoints*. Web. 24 May 2010.

"What Is the Average Reading Speed of Americans?" *Free Speed Reading*. n.p., n.d. Web. 8 August 2014.

"Why Outsource to India?" *Reasons to Outsource to India*. Outsorce2India.com. n.d. Web. 8 August 2014.

# Index

# About the Author

**Karen A. Wink** is an English professor at the U.S. Coast Guard Academy where she has taught composition and literature courses for twenty years. Previously, she taught high school English in Maryland for five years. The New England Association for Teachers of English (NEATE) awarded an "Excellence in Teaching" award to Dr. Wink. Her research focuses on rhetoric and pedagogy in the field of English Education.